THE JOY OF CHRIST'S COMING

From Traditional Religion

To Ageless Wisdom

HOWARD RAY CAREY

SHARE INTERNATIONAL FOUNDATION

Amsterdam, London, Los Angeles

Copyright © 1988 Howard Ray Carey, Arleta, CA

First Published in the Netherlands by
Share International Foundation
P.O. Box 41877, 1009 DB, Amsterdam
All rights reserved

ISBN 90-71484-04-1
ISBN 13 978-90-71484-04-9

This book is joyfully dedicated to the Christ and the Spiritual Hierarchy of our planet Earth, with gratitude for the generous help They beam to all disciples as we seek to transmit Their energies to a needy humanity.

Author's Note

These articles first appeared in *Share International* magazine, between February 1982 and December 1987.

Biblical quotations are taken from the Revised Standard version unless otherwise indicated.

Also By Howard Ray Carey

Journey Into Light and Joy (Marina del Rey, CA: De Vorss & Co., 1979)

Contents

Foreword... 1
1. From Traditional Religion To Ageless Wisdom........... 2
2. The Joy of Christ's Coming................................. 7
3. From Believing to Knowing — Our Unique Opportunity 17
4. Hidden Esoteric Wisdom in the Bible..................... 20
5. The Gates of the Temple................................... 27
6. Fire from Heaven... 32
7. Christmas of the Soul...................................... 36
8. The Choice Is Always Ours................................ 41
9. The Five-fold Path to Resurrection...................... 45
10. The Contribution of Religion in the New Age......... 49
11. Love: The Key to Sharing................................ 53
12. No Justice Without Sharing.............................. 57
13. Burning Away Barriers................................... 60
14. Release from Separatism and Pride..................... 63
15. A Christmas Message
The Sword of Cleavage — Herod vs. Christ............... 66
16. Our Voyage on the Sea of Life.......................... 70
17. Aquarian Age Good Samaritan........................... 73
18. Planetary Resurrection................................... 76
19. Inner Mysteries Revealed................................ 80
20. When the Walls Come Tumbling Down................ 83
21. A Time of Accounting.................................... 85
22. "I Come in Time"... 88
23. The Miracle of the Mustard Seed....................... 91
24. Written in Heaven.. 94
25. He Who Has Ears to Hear............................... 97

26. No Weeds Shall Grow..103
27. A Future Bathed in Light......................................106
28. A Present Day Parable on Karma and Forgiveness.......109
29. Hell or Heaven — We Make Our Own....................113
30. "That All Men May Quench Their Thirst"................116
31. Biblical Teachings and the Great Initiations.............. 120
32. The Second Initiation in the Bible..........................124
33. The Third Initiation: Transfiguration......................129
34. The Bible and the Great Renunciation.................... 134
35. The Fifth Initiation: Door to Mastership..................139
36. Music and Dancing... 143
37. Emergence from the Imprisoning Cave of Materialism..146
38. Yoke Fellows with Christ......................................150
39. The Life Cycle of Glamor and Illusion....................153
40. In All His Glory...156
41. Jacob's Ladder — And Ours................................ 159
42. Song and Prayer from Prison, at Midnight............... 162
43. Spiritual Healing — Past, Present and Future............165
44. Guerilla Warfare Ended Through Goodwill...............171
45. Commitment to Service..174
46. Banishing the Fear of Sharing................................177
47. The Glory of God...181
48. From Unlimited Revenge to Unconditional Love........184
49. A New Heart — A New World.............................189
50. What Is Fundamental?..192
51. Continuity of the Teaching in the Bible and In Our Day 196
The Great Invocation...201
References...203
Further Reading..204
Share International..206

Foreword

Howard Ray Carey is that unusual combination: a Methodist minister who is also a student of the esoteric teachings, and so can shine the revealing light of the esoteric tradition on the symbolic stories and events of the Christian Bible. His is thus a most valuable service. We have been privileged to publish these articles in the monthly magazine *Share International*, where they have rightly proved enormously informative and inspiring. We are glad to have the opportunity of presenting them in this collected form.

Benjamin Creme

1. From Traditional Religion To Ageless Wisdom

How does a Methodist minister become a convinced esotericist with a belief in the information about the presence and the work of Maitreya the Christ?

To begin with, let me state briefly where I was 35 years ago as an almost typical Methodist minister. Then I will try to outline some of the experiences which kept nudging me on toward where I am today. Back then, at 48 years of age, I was doing what I thought I could to promote world peace and human brotherhood. For example, I worked hard to bring about racial integration in the churches I served as pastor. Note that that was in the early days of church integration, when some Methodist church members thought it their duty to petition their bishop, seeking to get rid of such a radical pastor. Should I say that I have been 'out on a limb' before?

But I did not consider myself radical, even on social issues, just not as cautious as some. And on doctrinal matters I was pretty much 'middle of the road', to use a good Methodist phrase. Let me emphasize at the outset that I was definitely not a fundamentalist. A graduate of Garret School of Theology, a liberal Methodist seminary, here are some of the views I then held.

I believed in personal survival after death, but did not believe in any communication with people in that post-mortem state. Quite definitely I did not believe in the typical hell of fire and brimstone. For I could not conceive of a loving God permitting such a fate for some of His children. I thought there must be some opportunity for service and progress in the after-life, but was not at all open to the teaching of reincarnation. I used to argue this way: "Look, if I was John Jones in a previous life I don't remember a single thing about John. And if I'm going to be Timothy Smith in my next life, probably Tim won't remember anything about Howard Carey, so I do not see what sense it makes." Without going into too much detail about my pre-awakened self, let me mention one more matter. I had some faith in prayer, but not in spiritual healing.

So what are the experiences which began breaking down some of my prison walls to give me greater breathing space? First of all, in the church I was serving in Altadena, California, I got together for prayer a small group of interested persons. One of them brought a book on spiritual healing by Dr. John Gaynor Banks, a pioneer in reviving the practice of spiritual healing in 20th century Christendom. This Episcopal priest's book, entitled *Healing Everywhere*, outlined procedures and services for this form of healing. Soon members of the group began asking me to set up healing services. "What for," I thought, "what good would it do?" But I yielded to the pressure, established such services, and, after preliminaries, invited people to kneel at the altar rail for healing. Somewhat gingerly, as I remember it, I laid hands on them and prayed, really expecting nothing special to happen. But happen it did! They told me my hands were hot, and shared with me some definite improvements in health. Result: I have been acting as an instrument for spiritual healing ever since.

Next, a fellow minister showed me a book by Sherwood Eddy entitled *You Will Survive After Death*. I admired Dr. Eddy for his outstanding work for world peace. My question was: "Has Sherwood Eddy gone off his rocker?" Intrigued as I was, I was not about to invest my money in such a book, so I borrowed it. Eddy's evidential material concerning survival and communication was pretty convincing, so some light was beginning to stream through a window. About three years later I heard the famous medium Arthur Ford speak and was invited with a small group of ministers to his hotel room for a group seance. While in trance, Ford introduced my deceased aunt, Hat- tie Easterbrook, in such a startling way that I was convinced she was there, giving me encouragement in my ministry from 'the other side'. This was at a meeting sponsored by Spiritual Frontiers Fellowship, which had been established in 1956 to promote, in the churches, a deeper emphasis on prayer and meditation, spiritual healing, and evidences of survival.

After that experience I began attending SFF meetings as often as possible to see what I could learn. At the time Violet Stevens, widow of the deceased Episcopal Bishop Bertram Stevens, was in charge of study-meditation groups for Spiritual Frontiers Fellowship. Since I was a minister she kept asking me to start a study-meditation group in my home. Feeling quite un- prepared for that responsibility, I kept saying NO! For a while. But her persistence won out and in January 1964 I said: "Well, all right, I will try it." Result: I have been leading study-meditation groups in my home ever since. But now they are on a different level.

At first we were studying material like the books of Arthur Ford. This represented psychic realms at the higher levels of the astral plane. This was opening some doors, not always wisely, and I had many questions.

Three years later, in 1967, Edith Stauffer, head of High Point Foundation, introduced me to the Alice Bailey books, and to the School for Esoteric Studies in New York. Similar to the Arcane School, it has a most helpful correspondence course in the Ageless Wisdom which I pursued for several years. Perhaps you will have guessed that I quickly graduated from the Arthur Ford level of teaching, in the groups which were meeting with me, to the Master DK's[1] teaching through Alice Bailey. This of course opened many doors. I began to breathe free.

Then in 1980 Benjamin Creme came to Los Angeles for his first lecture here. Though I was not at the meeting, a member of my group was, and he brought me a copy of the first booklet available then about the reappearance of the Christ. At first reading it seemed a bit too far out. But the more I meditated on it and compared it to DK's teachings, the more convinced I became. So the next time Creme came to town I was right on hand to hear him and to experience the marvelous energies of the overshadowing of him by Maitreya. This left no doubts in my mind about the validity and unparalleled importance of these events, happening and to happen.

So in summary you can see that in my experience there has been no sudden blast of enlightenment, no blinding light such as Paul of Tarsus experienced on the Damascus road. Rather I have experienced a series of smaller steps, some taken with no hesitation, others with some fear and trembling. (What would my Methodist friends say, I wondered.) Years ago, when I first began a serious study of the inner life, I asked myself this question: "How can I know what to accept and what to reject?" The answer which came from my higher Self: accept what rings true to the law of love for all people. But, no matter what the inducements, steer clear of the glamorous traps of glittering psychic phenomena. For me this has proved to be a reliable guide.

For me now, as I approach my 84th birthday, I am profoundly grateful for all the help I have received from my higher Self and other great sources. Grateful that in so many areas I have received the help needed to step up from a belief system of the concrete mind to the level of true *knowing*, which no one can take from us. Grateful that, even though my physical energy is on the decrease, I do not feel that life is closing in on me, but rather that expanding vistas stretch out before me — both while I remain in this well-worn but still-serviceable body, and after I lay off this trench coat for finer garments. Grateful that I am able to have some small part — especially through Transmission Meditation[2] — in helping a bit toward the lifting of human consciousness to more adequate levels, thus helping a little in preparing the way for that great Day of Declaration of the World Teacher.

Finally, some may be surprised to learn that, though retired from the pastorate, I am still a Methodist minister, officially in good standing in this nine-million-member United Methodist Church. (Unofficially I wonder if I am still in 'good standing' with some Methodist friends who know a bit about my present views and work.) Be that as it may, I am able to share some insights of the Ageless Wisdom with the Sunday morning adult class I still teach at a nearby United Methodist congregation. And I am deeply grateful to United Methodism for the good fields of service it has provided, and continues to provide, for me, and for financial support as well.

Whatever our age, whatever our race, whatever our rays[3], let us join hands and hearts as we help prepare the way for that greatest day, and the greatest change in human life and history. Let us rejoice in the Christ's gracious invitation as he bids us: "Walk with Me into the sunlight of the New Time. Create with Me that glorious future for all."

September 1986

1. DK — Djwhal Khul, the Tibetan Master who gave His teachings through Alice A. Bailey.

2. Transmission Meditation was introduced to the world by Benjamin Creme's Master in 1974. It is a form of service rendered by transmitting Hierarchical energies into the world. See *Transmission — A Meditation for the New Age* by Benjamin Creme, published by Tara Center. (See "Further Reading," p. 204.)

3. The Seven Rays are seven great streams of Cosmic Energy originating in seven stars of the Great Bear. Their influence determines the nature and quality of all life. For further information see *A Treatise on the Seven Rays* by Alice A. Bailey, published by Lucis Press.

2. The Joy of Christ's Coming

Is the second coming of the Christ, or His reappearance, about to take place? Is He already here, in physical form, and soon to appear on international television, as some affirm? Certainly on radio and TV, and through books and sermons, we are being flooded with predictions of His imminent return. Many of these messages predict that He is coming to blast most of humanity, all but an elect few, with dismay, doom and destruction.

But fortunately there is also a far different kind of message coming to us — one of hope and joy, of goodwill, and peace. Certainly His coming in Palestine at the beginning of our era was heralded with glad tidings of joy and peace, by the heavenly host of angels, as recorded in the gospel of Luke. And we read that the father of John the Baptist looked to His coming, "When the day shall dawn upon us from on high, to give light to those who sit in darkness and in the shadow of death, to guide our feet into the way of peace." (Luke 1:78-9)

Some of us dare to believe that He is about to show His face to the whole world, and that again it is to be an occurrence to usher in joy, hope and peace. Even away back in the New Testament we have assurances to this effect. In the gospel accounts we find that Jesus foretold these crisis times at the end of the age — with wars, tumults, earthquakes, and all kinds of calamities — such as we are now having. Concerning this time He said: "When you see all this happening you may know that the kingdom of God is near." In that same passage, in verse 28 we read: "When all this begins to happen stand upright and hold your heads high, because your liberation is near." (Luke 21:31 and 28) And in John 15:11 we find that after speaking about the importance of abiding in him whatever comes, He states: "These things have I spoken unto you that my joy be in you, and that your joy may be full." These are just a few of the biblical passages which encourage us, in a time like this, to be joyful rather than depressed or gloomy.

This biblical emphasis of joy and gladness concerning His advent is echoed and re-echoed for us in our own twentieth century, both in the Tibetan's teachings given through Alice Bailey, and in the current writings of Benjamin Creme. In *The Reappearance of the Christ*, by Alice Bailey, we are told that happiness and joy represent a difficult lesson for us to learn. "It is for man a totally new experience and Christ will have to teach men how to handle happiness correctly, to overcome the ancient habits of misery, and thus to know the meaning of true joy." (p. 115)

And Creme's book, *Messages from Maitreya the Christ*, resounds with the emphasis of release from fear and the joy Christ has in store for us, which we can indeed emphasize right now. For instance, in Message No. 93 He states: "No man need fear for the future when My Shield is over him. No man need fear want when My Principle governs." And in Message No. 92: "My Message at this time of joyous celebration is this: awaken anew the love in the hearts of your brothers and teach them to share." Yes, again and again, as in Message No. 100, given on 19 March 1980, He emphasizes: "I am with you and in you. I am the heart of your life...I bring Joy."

As you can see, I am pointing out some of the parallels between what Christ emphasized 2,000 years ago and what is being given in this century. And I could find no more important note to start with than this theme of joy, the needed antidote for the great fear so prevalent today. For the more fully we can dwell in real joy, the better we can serve him, and help to usher in the new heaven, or at least the new earth, which God has promised, and which, even in the midst of the present crises, is in some ways beginning to manifest.

A second factor of note is the matter of the surprise element in His coming, seemingly 'too soon', at a time when He said:

"Therefore you must also be ready, for the Son of Man is coming at an hour you do not expect." (Matt. 24:44) And Paul warns us: "The day of the Lord will come like a thief."

Now let me quote some passages from Alice Bailey and Benjamin Creme, which also stress the imminence of His new appearance among us: "His hour has now come, because of the people's need in every land, and because of the invocative cry of the masses everywhere, and the advice of His disciples of all faiths and of all the world religions...When the Christ, the Avatar[1] of Love, makes His reappearance then will the sons of men who are now the Sons of God withdraw their faces from the shining light and radiate that light upon the sons of men who know not yet they are the Sons of God. Then shall the Coming One appear, His footsteps hastened through the valley of the shadow by the One of awful power Who stands upon the mountain top breathing out love eternal, light supernal, and peaceful silent Will. Then will the sons of men respond. Then will a newer light shine forth into the dismal, weary vale of earth. Then will new life course through the veins of men, and then will their vision compass all the ways of what may be. So peace will come again on earth, but a peace unlike aught known before. Then will the will-to-good flower forth as understanding, and understanding blossom as goodwill in men." (AAB, *Reappearance of the Christ*, p. 12-14)

In *Messages from Maitreya the Christ* we read: "Mankind has lost its way, and strayed far from the path prepared for it by God. Many there are now in the world who know this, who search and pray, and work towards the Light; but many more are blind and would rush towards disaster. My Plan is to halt this headlong plunge and to turn the tide." (Message No. 13)

Speaking of the shortness of the time before He plans to make His presence known world-wide, He states in Message No. 7: "My Aim is to shorten this time yet further, but an early declaration of My Presence depends on you, depends on your will to serve."

Now a third important matter concerned with His imminent appearance deals with what the Christ calls 'the sword of cleavage'. When He was here before He said: "Blessed are the peacemakers." But He said also: "Do not think that I have come to bring peace on earth; I have come to set a man against his father, and a daughter against her mother; and a man's foes will be those of his own household. He who loves father or mother more than me is not worthy of me; and he who loves son or daughter more than me is not worthy of me. He who finds his life will lose it, and he who loses his life for my sake will find it." (Matt. 10:34-9)

There is much misunderstanding about this. What it says to me is that if we are to be disciples, then the cause of Christ must take precedence over personal loyalties and considerations. The cleavage is caused by the fact that while some are ready to do this, others are not. It worked that way before. Bitter division arose between those who followed Him and those who rejected Him. And sometimes the division was between father and son, or mother and daughter.

Now we are told that the same will be true this time. On page 110 of Bailey's *Reappearance of the Christ* we read: "When He came before He said, I come not to bring peace but the sword. This will be true especially during the early days of His advent. The sword which He wields is the sword of the Spirit; it is that sword which produces cleavage between a true spirituality and an habitual materialism." Likewise in the book of Messages referred to before we read: "My coming brings Peace. Likewise, My Presence brings cleavage. My Sword, that Love which I am, will separate all men, will show the true from the false, will clear the way for the new Light which I bring. May it be that you can withstand this change, and accept My Light." (p. 156)

We also are given indication of the sources of what may be the greatest resistance. Consider these statements: "It is highly improbable that the reactionary churchmen will be the ones to recognize Him. He may appear in a totally unexpected guise; who is to say whether He will come as a politician, an economist, a leader of the people (arising from the midst of them), a scientist, or an artist." (*Reappearance of the Christ,* by AAB, p. 17)

And consider this: "The incredibly powerful international banking and financial institutions will prove to be among the last to accept the fact that a complete change in the world's financial and economic order is imperative. To meet this obstacle the Hierarchy has plans already made and ready to be put into effect. These involve the reconstruction of the world financial and economic order. A group of high initiates, themselves economists, industrialists and financial experts of great experience and achievement, are working with the Hierarchy, and have evolved a series of blueprints, alternative inter-related plans, which will solve the redistribution problems which are at the basis of the present world crisis. These can and will be speedily implemented when the need is seen and accepted... The cry for help and justice from the poor and starving nations will be too loud and dramatic to ignore." (*The Reappearance of the Christ and the Masters of Wisdom,* by B. Creme, p. 34)

These and other passages are given to assure us that, despite cleavage and resistance, the Plan and program of the Christ will win out against all opposition. Let me quote from the Messages just a few short paragraphs indicating firm assurance of the success of the Christ's mission after He openly appears among men: "My hope is — nay, My brothers, My knowledge is — that mankind will respond to My Call. I know this to be so. I know that within men sits a Divine Being, whose Plan it is that Love and Justice should triumph. This being so, the end is assured." (Message No. 77)

"The choice is man's alone. If he chooses the path which I shall indicate, that divinity shall verily shine forth. Otherwise, My brothers and sisters, the future for man would be fateful indeed. But, My friends, I know beforehand your answer and choice. Through your love — the love in your heart for your brothers — have no fear, My dear ones, you will choose correctly. This love will radiate throughout the world and on this you may count. My Presence guarantees that this shall be so. Already the changes are occurring in such magnitude that victory is assured." (Message No. 78)

In Message No. 65 we find this assurance couched in slightly different form: "Great, indeed, has been the enthusiasm of your brothers, which bodes well for the future of My Mission. When you, yourselves, see me, you will, I feel sure, respond likewise; for within you all does sit the same Light of Truth, of Justice and Freedom which I awaken in all who hear me. Therefore, My friends, have no fear that mankind will reject me. My Plans are safe in your hands."

The question is, I suppose, can we have the same strong assurance which He expresses? For myself, the more I meditate on this theme, the stronger my conviction becomes. Now before we go on to the next phase of our subject, let me quote from just one more of these strong assurances of the victory of His Plan. This one is from Message No. 44: "My Presence is causing such changes in the world that before long the knowledge of My existence will be ascertained...The divisions of old will merge and grow together; the sons of men will sense a higher Light and, turning their faces towards that Light, shall find My waiting to lead them. Thus shall it be. Thus shall the Truth in the hearts of men respond to the Truth which I am. Thus shall that new Light be kindled in their hearts, and the anguish of men depart."

Thus far we have looked briefly at the joy which belongs to us in connection with His coming at a time sooner than expected; at the sword of cleavage which He brings, and the resistance of vested interests and reactionary churchmen; also at some Messages of assurance that in spite of all resistance, He will be victorious.

Finally, let us consider a few of the changes which are to take place because of His world-wide appeal, and what our part is to be in these world-shaking changes. Going back again to the Bible, we find in II Peter 3:13 the promise of "a new heaven and a new earth in which righteousness dwells." To see what this new quality of life on earth is to be like, let us look further. We find a beautiful symbolic portrayal of it in the closing chapters of the Book of Revelation, chapters 21 and 22. Let me quote a few selected verses from those chapters:

"I saw a new heaven and a new earth...and the sea was no more. And I saw the holy city, the new Jerusalem [meaning the place of peace — HRC] coming down out of heaven from God, prepared as a bride adorned for her husband; and I heard a great voice from the throne saying, 'Behold the dwelling of God is with men. He will dwell with them and they shall be his people, and God himself will be with them; He will wipe away every tear from their eyes, for the former things have passed away.'

"And I saw no temple in the city, for its temple is the Lord God the Almighty and the Lamb [Christ — HRC]...Then he showed me the river of the water of life, bright as crystal, flowing from the throne of God and of the Lamb, through the middle of the street of the city; also, on either side of the river the tree of life with its twelve kinds of fruit, yielding its fruit each month; and the leaves of the tree were for the healing of the nations." The symbolism flows on, but this is perhaps sufficient to show the beauty and newness of life when God and the Lamb, or Christ, are openly with us.

Now let us take a look at some more recent words, giving further indication as to what this new world is to be like, through the influence of Christ's active presence on the physical plane. First from AAB's *The Reappearance of the Christ* (page 101):

"Thus the Christ, with the fused energies of love and wisdom, with the aid of the Avatar of Synthesis[2] and the Buddha[2], and under the influence of the Spirit of Peace and of Equilibrium², can implement and direct the energies which will produce the coming new civilization. He will see, demonstrating before His eyes, the true resurrection — the emergence of mankind from the imprisoning cave of materialism. Thus He will 'see of the travail of His soul and shall be satisfied.' "

Turning again to the Messages, we find in so many of them the emphasis on love, brotherhood, justice and sharing. "My energy of Love, My Gift, creates among men a pool of happiness. Dip deeply therein, My friends and, shining with the Light of Love emerge into a New Day... The rock upon which that glorious future will be built is Love, Justice and Sharing." (Message No. 45)

"The world awaits the sounding of the Cosmic Dates. The nations prepare for a New Dispensation, and in Trust and Brotherhood all men will share." (Message No. 36)

"I shall show you wonders of which you cannot dream. I shall release from your eyes the blindfold of ignorance. I shall drive from this earth forever the curse of hatred, the sin of separation... The time is coming, My friends, when the Light of Truth shall shine all around you, when man shall take his brother to his heart and know him as himself." (Message No. 51)

We are not led to expect that all these great changes will take place overnight, but that His coming will bring a great change, a definite turning point from chaos toward harmony and goodwill. So, perhaps more rapidly than we can conjecture, the present difficulties will be transmuted into tranquility and peace. Let me quote from Creme's *The Reappearance of the Christ and the Masters of Wisdom* (p. 177) a surprisingly strong statement to that effect: "He works very closely with the law of action and reaction, and His function is to transform the prevalent discord, confusion, chaos, turmoil in the world into its opposite, so that we shall enter an era of tranquility and peace — in exact proportion to the present discord. The violence and hatred of today will be transmuted into goodwill, and again, in exact proportion to the intensity of the hatred and violence. This is the great law of action and reaction. The law stated is that action and reaction are equal and opposite; and this great entity, the Spirit of Equilibrium, is working now with the Christ, producing the transformation of the world."

Thus far we have seen a few minor hints as to our part in all this. Let us now look a bit more closely into what is intended as our share and our responsibility. "Take now the first steps into your glory. Serve the purpose of your return and the Plan of God; they are one and the same. My Masters will show you the first steps out of the quagmire. They will show you that a simpler life can be led in full happiness and manifested Divinity, through Love and Service of our brothers...Make now your choice: to serve My Plan and see the Light which beckons you into the future, or to sound forever the knell of regret." (Message No. 16)

"My coming will transform the world, but the major work of restoration must be done by you. I am the Architect, only, of the Plan. You, My friends and brothers, are the willing builders of the shining Temple of Truth. I shall give you the key of that Temple, and entering therein shall you know God. My Masters await, also, your response to their guidance. Give them your trust and let them lead you into the New Dawn, sharing together the earth's produce, knowing together the joy of Brotherhood, manifesting together the divinity within you all. The time is short indeed till you shall see me. Make best use of this little time to prepare My Way, to teach all those whom you meet the words of Truth which I send you. Lead them, too, into the Path of Light and the Promise which My return brings to the world. My emergence into full vision is imminent. Watch and wait and sleep not." (Message No. 65)

Let me give you one more quote from the Messages, this one from Message No. 50:

"Take Me to your hearts, as I, My dear brothers and sisters, have taken you to mine, and working together let us remake the world. Let us change all that is corrupt and useless in your structures, all that prevents the manifestation of your divinity. Let us together show the way for the Little Ones and hold fast the world for them. I appeal to you to aid Me in My Task of succour... My coming is planned, is lawful, and releases to you the Love and Will of God.

I am the Manifestation of both Love and Will.

I am the Caretaker.

I am the One sent to teach you.

I am the Flute Player...

I am the Lawgiver.

I hear all pleas.

I come to Save.

I render Service.

Make yourselves one with me, and let us together serve the Plan...

May the Divine Light and Love and Power of the One Most Holy God be now manifest within your hearts and minds. May this Light and Love and Power lead to the manifestation of that Divine Being Whom in truth you are.''

February 1982

1. Avatar — Spiritual Being who 'descends' in answer to mankind's call and need.

2. Avatar of Synthesis — the Buddha — the Spirit of Peace and of Equilibrium. Three Great Beings who constitute a triangle of Cosmic Energies, reinforcing and strengthening the energies of the Christ.

3. From Believing to Knowing — Our Unique Opportunity

Long ago the Christ, speaking through His disciple Jesus, said: "If you continue in my word, you are truly my disciples, and you will know the truth, and the truth will make you free." (John 8:31-2) Do we realize what a great promise this is? Too often we have equated knowing with mere belief. But in reality there is a vast difference between the two. Belief is of the lower mind, and often is swept away by a torrent of opposing 'logic'. But real knowing is a bringing through of truth from the high level of the intuition. Thus what we know in this true sense "no man takes from us," as was promised long ago. Truly, the realization we bring through from the higher Self is unshakable knowing. What a contrast to mere believing, which is like the proverbial house built on the shifting sands.

What has this to do with the reappearance of the Christ, we may ask. I would say that it has much to do with the security of our grasp of this truth, and our holding to it. Of course, even the belief in His imminent declaration is an important start. And I confess that a couple of years ago when I first heard this teaching through Benjamin Creme, I felt somewhat skeptical but somewhat believing. And the more I tuned in on it through reading, pondering and meditation, the more fully it became, not merely an article of faith, but of deep intuitive realization.

And all of us who are disciples of the Christ, through whatever form of faith, can have this greater certainty — far greater than whatever belief we may have started with. The above quotation from the gospel of John is a promise that if we are willing to pay the price of discipline — the cost of discipleship — we will really know this liberating truth which sets us free.

In this liberating truth let us rejoice in the unique opportunity which is ours: the opportunity to know ahead of time that the

Christ is about to make His very presence known to us and to all the world. How our hearts leap with joy as we contemplate this fulfillment of the promise made in the first century: "I will see you again, and your hearts will rejoice, and no one will take your joy from you." (John 16:22)

As He pointed out in His Message No. 65, we have the thrilling opportunity to be co-workers with him in building the shining Temple of Truth in this world in which we live. "My coming will transform this world, but the major work of restoration must be done by you. I am the Architect, only, of the Plan. You, My friends and brothers, are the willing builders of the shining Temple of Truth." Have we perhaps thought that such an opportunity — such a privilege — would be open only to Masters of Wisdom and high initiates? Let us rejoice that this opportunity is open to all of us who are ready to be "willing builders" of this shining temple of humanity.

This challenge is further reinforced in other Messages. For example, in Message No. 94 He asks again for our willing help: "Without your willing help naught may be done. I come to lead and teach, not to enforce. Take, then, to your hearts this, My Appeal, and work with Me, for your brothers, and so save the world."

Dare we believe that He is calling us to be with him co-saviors of the world? Can we go farther than mere belief, and know — realize in ourselves — that this is our calling, our opportunity? Let us ponder the great work we have to do under His leadership. But, lest we be overwhelmed by this challenge, let us ponder too all the empowering help He is offering us. For He says: "Take within you that which I am, and prepare to see a new Light. Hold within you that which I give, and know the meaning of Truth. Release within you that which you eternally are, and become gods." (Message No. 80) If it takes our breath away to have him calling us gods, it is good to recall that this is but echoing what He said through Jesus long ago: "Is it not written in your law, 'I said, you are gods'? If he called them gods to whom the word of God came...do you say of him whom the Father consecrated and sent into the world, 'You are blaspheming' because I said 'I am the Son of God'? If I am not doing the works of my Father, then do not believe me; but if I do them, then even though you do not believe me, believe the works, that you may know and understand that the Father is in me and I am in the Father." (John 10:34-38) Isn't this exactly what He is saying today: that He is first giving His message of sharing, justice, brotherhood, and love, so that He may be known by His "works" rather than on some emotional basis of an outmoded devotion?

This emphasis on sharing, justice, brotherhood, and love is like a powerful refrain, running through His appeal to us, and pointing up another facet of our unique opportunity, another facet of the diamond of our joy, as we begin now to share, and to make known His requirements of sharing, justice, brotherhood and love. Let us share our joy; let us gladly share our resources — physical, emotional, mental, and spiritual. Let us do our part to make known among all nations and the United Nations the beauty of this, Maitreya's great solution to the problems of mankind.

April 1982

4. Hidden Esoteric Wisdom in the Bible

Someone has asked: "Why on earth did Christian teaching not bear any relevant information in relation to esoteric knowledge, to reincarnation, etc.?" Another form in which this question is put to us is this: "Which are the hidden biblical clues? Where flows the esoteric stream beneath the surface of the Bible?"

Perhaps the first question should be slightly re-worded to read: "Why did Christian teaching not bear any *obvious* information relating to esoteric knowledge, including reincarnation?" This comes nearer the mark. For the Bible is full of esoteric wisdom. But it may take some insight to discover it. It seems to be the case, especially in the past, that esoteric information, when embodied in literature made available to the public, was veiled beneath exoteric or more obvious interpretations.

For if the deep symbolic meanings in biblical literature had been made obvious, on the surface, it is questionable whether the Bible could have survived, especially through the dark ages. It probably would have been discarded as irrelevant.

It seems to be an indication of genius on the part of many writers, whose works later were gathered together to make up the Bible, that they produced material which could be interpreted on at least three different levels. The first level is of course a quite literal one. The second is a bit more sophisticated but still subject to interpretation by the concrete mind of the orthodox religionist. The third carries an esoteric meaning.

Let us take as an example one of the best known and most loved of Jesus' parables, that of the prodigal son, found in Luke 15:11-32. Looking at this from a very literal perspective one might explain it as a warning about what happens to a reckless youth, one who demands everything he can get from his father, and squanders it all on drugs and 'women'. Then he ends up broke and feeding pigs (the ultimate humiliation for a Jew of that time), and finally comes crawling back to dad in a state of near starvation.

A second but still fairly obvious interpretation which might be made by a traditional churchman could be: Here is the rebellion of youth, striking out against parental authority. The youth sinks into a life of flagrant 'sin'. But sometime before death he accepts Christ, becomes converted — so he is saved from hell, and the father (God) welcomes him to heaven following death.

The third level of interpretation, though there may be many variations, sees it this way: The son, leaving home and traveling to the far country, indicates the Soul or higher Self on the involutionary spiral of experience — finally sinking into the deepest possible involvement in matter. In that mess he finally discovers that the pleasures and rewards of materialism leave him deeply hungry for a more satisfying life. Thus he comes to some measure of realization of himself. Then he begins the long journey of many lifetimes back to the 'father's house' (the Monad), the home of the Soul.

In this interpretation the older brother can represent the devic or angelic line of evolution. How meaningful to us, then, is the closing word of the Father: "This, your brother, was dead, and is alive. He was lost and is found." Can we not see that the wayward son represents all of us in the human race — at one point or another either on the trek to the far country to feed the animal nature — or on the long, long journey back home!

If we read the 13th chapter of Matthew with open eyes we find that Jesus' disciples were deeply puzzled as to why he spoke to the curious crowds in these word pictures, with such deeply hidden meanings. So they put the question to Jesus. He replied: "This is why I speak to them in parables, because seeing they do not see, and hearing they do not hear, nor do they understand." But He was planting the good seed deep in their lives to ponder upon, so that hopefully some time it would sprout, grow, and as He suggested "bring forth grain, some a hundred fold, some sixty, some thirty." (All significant numbers, symbolically, no doubt.)

But to His disciples Jesus said: "Blessed are your eyes, for they see, and your ears, for they hear." As you and I read the Bible let us ask ourselves: How acute is our esoteric vision and hearing?

Geoffrey Hodson, a theosophical writer, in his book *The Hidden Wisdom in the Holy Bible,* Vol. I, gives us excellent clues to the symbolic meanings of the Bible. One of his suggestions is that we look at many biblical passages not for historical information, but that we consider them as happenings within our lives.

Take, for instance, the account given in Mark 4:35-41. It is the story of Jesus and His disciples caught in a severe storm on the Sea or Lake of Galilee. The boat seemed in danger of sinking. Jesus was asleep in the stern of the boat, when His disciples, in panic, awakened him. He asked, "Why are you afraid? Have you no faith?" He is reported to have calmed both the sea and the disciples by His word. Those who look at this as an historical incident sometimes argue as to whether the water becoming calm was a natural phenomenon, or whether Jesus used super-normal power to still the raging waves.

But let us look at it as having an important hidden meaning as an inner happening within us. Let the waters of the sea represent the sea of life over which we are making our life's voyage; the boat, our lower self or body; the raging storm, the emotional disturbances we may encounter; the disciples, the many aspects of our consciousness. The most important passenger in our boat — our life — is the Christ within. Why do we wait until some crisis seems to threaten us before awakening this Christ consciousness? But when this Christ life is awakened within us, what power it has to quiet the surging billows of our emotions — including the fears aroused by life's threatening storms!

The initiate Paul gives a number of clues about this hidden wisdom. In writing to the church at Corinth he says: "I fed you with milk, not solid food, for you were not ready for it, and even yet you are not ready." (1 Cor. 3:2) "Yet among the mature we do impart wisdom. We impart a secret and hidden wisdom of God, which God decreed before the ages for our glorification...What no eye has seen, nor ear heard, nor the heart of man conceived, what God has prepared for those who love him, God has revealed to us through the Spirit. For the Spirit searches everything, even the depths of God." (1 Cor. 2:6-7,9-10) In 1 Thes. 5:23 Paul mentions what the Master DK calls our three periodic vehicles: Spirit, Soul and body.

And in his second letter to the Corinthians Paul refers to out-of-body experience as well as to the third level of the heavenly or inner life: "I know a man in Christ who fourteen years ago was caught up to the third heaven — whether in the body or out of the body I do not know, God knows. And I know that this man was caught up into Paradise... And he heard things which cannot be told, which man may not utter." (2 Cor. 12:2-4) Note that here we have reference to inner truths too esoteric to be put into print or to repeat orally.

In the Jerusalem Bible translation — more accurate than most — Paul reports going through an initiation: "I know how to be poor and I know how to be rich too. I have been through my initiation and now I am ready for anything anywhere; full stomach or empty stomach, poverty or plenty. There is nothing I cannot master with the help of the One who gives me strength." (Phil. 4:11-13)

Space does not permit setting forth in detail the many esoteric references found in other parts of the Bible, but let us look at a few of them, such as the creation story in Genesis, with the inner meanings of Adam and Eve as the masculine and feminine principles of our personalities; the garden of Eden, the experience which every baby repeats in his earliest years; symbolic meanings of the serpent, and the fruit of the tree of knowledge of good and evil, and the tree of life; primitive man driven from the Paradise of Eden, as every baby — unless retarded — has to leave babyhood behind.

Look at the story of Noah, the ark, and the deluge (Atlantis destroyed). Note Abraham visited by angels; Abraham paying tribute or tithe to Melchizedek, king of Salem (peace), priest of the most high God, referred to by the writer as a being "having neither beginning of days nor end of life, but made like unto the Son of God." (Obviously an avatar.)

Think of Elijah, with his super-normal power to call down fire from 'heaven' to consume the water-soaked wood, as well as the offering on the altar; Elijah coming out from the cave, where he had hidden, as you and I sometimes do; coming out to the mouth of the cave, where he witnessed the earthquake, wind and fire; but found God speaking to him through the 'still small voice within'; later that same prophet escaping the usual process of death through being caught up to heaven in a chariot of fire.

Elijah is followed by Elisha, who saves the day for the king of Israel by his powers of telepathy and clairvoyance. He also brings the guerilla warfare of the time to an end through his wisdom. Think of Shadrach, Meshach and Abednego being thrown into the seven times overheated fiery furnace. Are we not all subjected to this on the burning ground when preparing for initiation? In the fiery furnace a fourth being is seen with them "walking in the midst of the fire." They came out unscathed and "no smell of fire had come upon them." Can we come through our testings with no hint of the fire we have been through?

What about the Virgin Mary being impregnated — not by Joseph, the rational mind — but by the Spirit? And Herod, symbolic ruler of the lower self, seeking to kill the new-born Christ, just as the 'Herod' in us seeks to kill off the growing Christ consciousness, because the lower self is ever jealous and fearful of having its reign snatched away.

Then there is the greatest esoteric account in the Bible: the crucifixion of Jesus, followed by His coming forth from the tomb in a resurrected body. Isn't this the experience we all must eventually go through: death and re-birth on higher levels? And the Bible has so many more esoteric treasures.

Though we cannot report on these scores of other esoteric matters, we must say a word about reincarnation. In the eleventh chapter of Matthew we find Jesus saying: "Truly I say to you, among those born of women there has arisen no-one greater than John the Baptist. Yet he who is least in the kingdom of heaven is greater than he." (Matt. 11:11) Take note that those merely born of women have not yet undergone the spiritual birth of first initiation. But those who are least in the Kingdom of Heaven, the fifth kingdom, have had the first initiation. Two verses later, following the Jerusalem Bible, we find Jesus emphasizing: "And he (John the Baptist) if you will believe me, is the Elijah who was to return. If anyone has ears to hear, let him listen."

Again in Matthew 17 after the account of the transfiguration —a symbolic portrayal of the third initiation —we have a similar reference to John the Baptist as Elijah: "The disciples put this question to him. Why do the scribes say that Elijah must come first? True, he replied...however I tell you that Elijah has come already and they did not recognize him. The disciples then understood that he had been speaking of John the Baptist." (Matt. 17:10-13)

In Revelation 3:12 we read: "He who conquers I will make him a pillar in the temple of my God. Never shall he go out of it." Some of us understand this to mean that he who conquers is one who has worked out all his karma, and thus does not need to go out into any further incarnation.

So as we read the Bible let us perceive it with seeing eyes and inner understanding. The Christ indicates that when we do that we will discover the pearl of great price. Can we sense the inner meaning of this? When we make that discovery we will be ready to give up all our accumulated treasures for this One Great Jewel! Are we ready?

August 1982

5. The Gates of the Temple

Have you heard the inspiring anthem sometimes sung in Christian churches: "Open the Gates of the Temple, and the King of Glory shall come in?" It seems to be based on a stirring passage in the 24th Psalm: "Lift up your heads, O ye gates, and be ye lifted up, ye everlasting doors, and the King of Glory shall come in."

Prior to studying the Ageless Wisdom I presumed this referred only to a temple made with human hands, such as Solomon's temple in Jerusalem. Now, however, I get a glimpse of a metaphysical or esoteric meaning. In Paul's first letter to the Corinthians, in the third chapter, he asks a poignant question: "Do you not know that you are the temple of God, and that the spirit of God dwells in you?"

Now if one's body is a temple of God, what are its gates or doors? In the dense physical body these would be the eyes, ears, nostrils, mouth, plus the anal and urinary orifices. But we know now that the dense body is not the sum total of our physical nature; for that includes also the important etheric counterpart, designated variously as the etheric body, etheric double, vital body, or energy body. It has many minor doors or etheric centers. And, of vast importance, seven major centers or chakras. Five of these are in the etheric spine, and two in the head.

Some writers list these seven centers as follows: the base center, spleen center, solar plexus, heart center, throat center, ajna or third eye center, and head or crown center. In such a listing the center at the base of the spine and the one just above it, the sacral center (related to the sex glands) are lumped together as if they constituted but one chakra. But the Master DK, writing through Alice Bailey, makes a clear distinction between the base center and the sacral center. So His listing is: base center, sacral center, solar plexus, heart, throat, ajna and head centers. How about the spleen center, then? He recognizes it as an important chakra for receiving and distributing pranic[1] energy. But He does not list it as one of the major seven because it is not so vitally related to the transmutation of our energies as we develop spiritually. There is a long process of the gradual lifting of energies from the three centers below the diaphragm to the four above the diaphragm.

Now let us look at the biblical references already given, in relation to these centers. And we may well ask: "Was the writer of the 24th Psalm clairvoyant?" If so he no doubt could see the vast difference between the individual who is not developed spiritually, on the one hand, and a person on the path of discipleship, with regard to the condition of those chakras. For teachers of the Inner Wisdom tell us that, to clairvoyant vision, an unopened center appears like a closed bud, with the unopened flower bending downward. But when a center is vivified an open lotus is seen, pointing upward. What an appropriate esoteric phrasing then is the Psalmist's word: "Lift up your heads O ye gates, and be ye lifted up ye everlasting doors."

Then comes the statement: "And the King of Glory shall come in." In response to the question "Who is this King of Glory?" the answer comes: "The Lord of Hosts. He is the King of Glory." So, who is the King of Glory in your life and mine? Obviously our own higher nature, our true being. This is first seen as the Soul, and later as the Monad or Spirit, the divine ever-living Spark.

So here we have an example of a biblical passage with significant meanings on at least two levels of understanding. To the usual worshipper this Psalm about opening the gates of the temple and the King of Glory coming in carries an inspiring thought about a temple or church opening up wide so that "whosoever will may come." The climber on life's mountain might appreciate this level of meaning as being of value to many. But in addition he may perceive the much deeper meaning of the chakras or centers opening in a beautiful way to admit the light and love and power of the higher nature — right here on the physical plane.

Quite a number of groups and individuals, thinking of the wonder and beauty of the light which can enter when the centers are properly opened, are these days concentrating on the base center, seeking by diligent effort to raise the serpent (kundalini) fire up the spine to the head center. Here is where we need a strong word of caution. For if the opening of the centers is forced, either through drugs or meditation on the centers, much harm can be done. For the kundalini can rush up to the brain before there is readiness for it, and thus cause brain damage; or it can rush into the sex glands and produce the extreme kind of sexual pressure which no amount of sex can satisfy. And drug abuse often produces so many holes or tears in the protective etheric web that the individual falls prey to a great variety of entities on the lower astral planes which may decide to come in and take up residence, sometimes taking over control of the individual's thoughts and actions in ways which produce most distressing consequences. Such damage is extremely hard to repair.

Let us take note of just a few of the many urgent words of warning which the Tibetan Master issues through the Alice Bailey books: "The whole subject of the centres is dangerous if misunderstood; the centres constitute a menace when prematurely awakened or unduly energised." (*The Rays and the Initiations*, p. 336)

"I sound here a solemn word of warning. Let a man apply himself to a life of high altruism, to a discipline that will refine and bring his lower vehicles into subjection, and to a strenuous endeavour to purify and control his sheaths. When he has done this, and has both raised and stabilised his vibration, he will find that the development and functioning of the centres has pursued a parallel course, and that (apart from his active participation) the work has proceeded along the desired lines. Much danger and dire calamity attends the man who arouses these centres by unlawful methods, and who experiments with the fires of his body without the needed technical knowledge. He may, by his efforts, succeed in arousing the fires and in intensifying the action of the centres, but he will pay the price of ignorance in the destruction of matter, in the burning of bodily or brain tissue, in the development of insanity, and in opening the door to currents and forces, undesirable and destructive...In these matters concerning the subjective life, it is the part of discretion to move with caution and with care. The aspirant, therefore, has three things to do:

1. Purify, discipline and transmute his threefold lower nature.

2. Develop knowledge of himself, and equip his mental body; build the causal body by good deeds and thoughts.

3. Serve the race in utter self-abnegation.

In doing this he fulfills the law, he puts himself in the right condition for training, fits himself for the ultimate application of the Rod of Initiation, and thus minimises the danger that attends awakening of the fire." (*A Treatise on Cosmic Fire*, p. 162)

Again in this same Psalm we find indication of needed preparation for the opening of doors and the coming in of the Lord of Glory. Verse 3: "Who shall ascend the hill of the Lord? And who shall stand in his holy place?" [High consciousness — HRC] Verses 4 and 5: "He who has clean hands and a pure heart; who does not lift up his soul to what is false, and does not swear deceitfully. He will receive blessing from the Lord and vindication from the God of his salvation."

So let us be grateful that we have both warning and promise. Warning of the dangers of opening the centers through drugs or through concentration on the centers. And assurance of the beauty of the higher way, as we take the path of discipline, of dedication to the highest we know, of prayer and meditation, and of evoking Soul love and light for the serving of humanity.

Then the doors of the temple will be properly opened from within, under divine direction of the Soul and the Hierarchy. And the indwelling King of Glory will come into the physical temple. Then the results will be health, fulfillment, light and joy, and eventually bliss.

September 1982

1. Pranic/Prana —energy streaming from the sun which imbues all life with vitality.

6. Fire From Heaven

In the 18th chapter of the First Book of Kings, in the Bible, we find a graphic description of a crucial contest between two opposed religious groups of that time. On the one hand we have Elijah, presented as a great prophet of the true God, the Yahweh (Jehovah) Deity of Israel. Opposed to him were said to be 450 prophets or priests of Baal. These were representatives of a fertility religion in which child sacrifice was practiced, as well as animal sacrifices. Both types of sacrifice were offered up to the Baals in order to ensure fertility of flocks and herds, and abundance of crops.

Such practices were vehemently opposed by such men as Elijah. Their tradition went back to Abraham, the original Hebrew patriarch. According to the account in Genesis, Abraham was ready to slay his son Isaac, to satisfy what were thought to be the demands of Deity for sacrifice to him of what was most precious. At that crucial moment God provided a lamb in the thicket as a substitute for the child, and Isaac was spared. From that time on, supposedly, the Hebrew people were strongly against child sacrifice, but it did happen at times.

The setting of the contest portrayed in the First Book of Kings was this: Israel's King Ahab had established a political alliance with the neighboring king of Tyre. As part of the deal Ahab married a Phoenician princess, Jezebel, daughter of Ethbaal, priest-king of Tyre and Sidon. Jezebel is pictured as a scheming, evil woman of great power and cunning. (Perhaps a powerful first-ray personality?[1]) In the Book of Revelation, written almost a thousand years later, the author refers to a woman in one of the churches of the time as "that Jezebel who...is teaching and beguiling my servants to practice immorality, and to eat food sacrificed to idols." And in our own day, to call a woman a Jezebel is to label her as the epitome of evil.

This Jezebel of Elijah's day was an ardent promoter of her native religion of Baal worship. She appeared to have the passive consent of King Ahab as she almost obliterated the leadership of Israel's worship of Yahweh. And she had gathered around her a cult of 450 prophet-priests of Baal.

Elijah, perhaps also a first-ray personality1, could tolerate the situation no longer. Through King Ahab he challenged all the leaders of the Baal cult to meet him on Mount Carmel. There they were to prepare a burnt offering of a bull, to be offered up to their deity, Baal, and without lighting the wood on the altar were to call down fire from heaven to consume the offering. They cried long and loud to Baal to come and perform this miracle. They even slashed themselves to let their blood flow, indicating their commitment to self-sacrifice.

When nothing happened, Elijah ridiculed them. Then he prepared another bull for sacrifice on an altar dedicated to God (Yahweh). He had his assistants pour several buckets of water over the whole thing. Then he called on God to send fire from heaven, which came down and consumed the animal flesh, water, wood and stone. This is pictured as a great victory of true religion and complete defeat for the kind of base religion which would offer up children as burnt offerings to appease some deity.

We can make of this what we will. The Ageless Wisdom teachings, which come to us through people like Alice Bailey, Benjamin Creme and others, indicate that very high initiates have real power over nature, being able to control it in surprising ways — always for worthy purposes. Was Elijah such a high initiate? Did he have such powers as seem to be indicated in this account and as portrayed in other Old Testament accounts of him? Or was this narrative, written in its present form about a hundred years later, greatly exaggerated or largely symbolic?

It is not for me to try to determine for you whether to take this account literally or otherwise. But however we 'stack it' perhaps we can see an important parallel with the world crisis of our civilization today. The Baal worshippers of that day were materialists seeking a selfish abundance of crops and livestock for their own separative group or tribe. And they were willing to sacrifice even their own children for that end! Is not the same thing happening today?

Who are the priests and prophets of 'Baal' in our time? What about those who predict that if we will just raise the separative nationalistic walls of tariffs and armaments higher, we will have returning prosperity for ourselves — never mind the rest of the world. And do we not see child sacrifice in many places: in the slaughter of the innocents in Lebanon and many other places, and in the starving of millions of children in Africa and so many parts of Asia?

Some are deluded into thinking that nuclear bombs and warheads provide the needed heavenly fire for today. But is it not evident that these are very earthly products, the means of selfish and foolhardy destruction?

Where are the modern counterparts of Elijah? Surely they are the high initiates, the Masters of Wisdom, and the World Teacher, who come with the true fire from 'heaven'. What then is this fire? We have learned that such fire is an important symbol of the power of the high mental (or heavenly) planes. These Great Ones are now bringing it down to earth — to the physical plane — to obliterate all our selfish, separative altars; where we so foolishly have been offering up our substance, our sons and daughters, and often ourselves! This we have done in a vain attempt to bring the 'fertility' of prosperity to our party or nation, at the expense of God's children on the other side of the fence we have erected.

It is for each of us to decide the particular way in which our own resources, our substance, our energy, our meditation, and our activities are to be offered in co-operation with the Great

Ones. But let us be fully aware that our substance, our meditation, our energy and our service are urgently needed right now in co-operation with the Christ and the Masters. The need is so great that we had best beware. If we hang back and hesitate to enlist with them, in accordance with our best guidance and wisdom, then are we not unwittingly in league with the modern 'Baals' of our day?

That which Maitreya has called the sword of cleavage is cutting pretty deep today. The issue is the survival of humanity on this planet. And, beyond survival, the building of the way of sharing, love, justice and brotherhood for all God's children here on planet earth. Here where we still have to demonstrate in joyous, sacrificial living the meaning of the truth that we are indeed all one! What is the true meaning of this oneness? Only in united and joyous sharing, brotherhood and love will we find the puzzle solved. Each of us has to face the question: can God and humanity count on you and on me to exert all our weight — not as slight as imagined — on the side of the light, love and power which is the true fire from heaven?

In love, in trust and in knowing that, "Life is ever Lord of death, and love can never lose its own," let us give ourselves gladly and fully. Then the living fire will ignite us as radiant torches of light, with power to dispel darkness, and to bring the long-awaited New Day.

November 1982

1. Readers may be interested to learn the following ray structures, provided by Benjamin Creme's Master, of Elijah and Jezebel. Elijah — 2nd ray soul, 1st ray personality (well-integrated and infused), 1st ray mental body, 6th ray astral body, 1st ray physical body. Jezebel — 1st ray soul, 6th ray personality, 3rd ray mental body, 6th ray astral body, 3rd ray physical body.

7. Christmas of the Soul

That which we celebrate at Christmas, if we have insight, is not so much an event which took place in Palestine in an ancient time, but rather an event, which in both ancient and present times transpires within the human heart — when the individual is spiritually prepared for it. It is an inner drama — you could call it a Soul drama. Paradoxically, it is an event rooted in the infinite, but finding expression in the finite. It has its source in the timeless, yet it transpires at a given moment in time. It is a universal reality, yet it happens within the human heart.

It is called the first initiation. There are five major initiations leading from the human kingdom, or human level of life, to the spiritual level, the Kingdom of God. And Christmas celebrates the first of these five. (The second is called the Baptism — into greater responsibility; the third, the Transfiguration; the fourth, the complete Renunciation or Crucifixion; and the fifth, the Resurrection into full citizenship in the spiritual kingdom, or Mastership.[1])

Christmas, as celebrated in most churches, is clothed in the garments of Christian theology and the trappings of Christian creed. As celebrated commercially, it is wrapped in tinsel and toys — toys like scotch whiskey and fur pieces and stuffed stomachs.

There is a truer way of understanding it, and a better way of celebrating it. On this level we know that this truth which Christmas means is not the exclusive property of any one religion. Parenthetically, it is interesting to note that the events of that first Christmas did not take place among Christians at all, because Christianity had not yet been established. All the members of the 'holy family' were, of course, Jews. But they do not have a corner on Christmas either, for, if we just knew it, all families are holy. So, that which we celebrate at this season really belongs to all.

It is a drama of the inner life. So we are not concerned about those modern Bible scholars who maintain that the birth stories concerning Jesus, which appear in different versions and only in Matthew and Luke, are later additions to the gospel. As a drama of the inner life, what matters is not whether there was, on the physical plane, a virgin birth, a new star in the outer sky, and shepherds and wise men. They do, however, represent symbols of inner truths, and this is the reality with which we are concerned.

To begin with, what is the meaning of this new birth pictured as taking place in a stable among cattle and other animals? Some would reply, "Because that is where Jesus was actually born." Possibly He was, but we have no need to enter into that dispute. What the birth in the stable among the animals really symbolizes is the fact that this initiation, or New Birth, takes place while we are incarnate in a physical or animal body, not while we are on the higher planes between incarnations. It may take place at night while we are on another level of consciousness, and so perhaps be out of the body temporarily, but this divine life has to take root and grow right here in the heart center of this physical or animal life.

Next, we are told that Joseph was not the real father of Jesus, but instead that Mary was impregnated by the overshadowing Spirit. The biblical literalist insists that it definitely was an immaculate conception and a virgin birth, but on the level we are viewing these matters it does not matter one way or the other. On the higher level, Joseph represents the concrete or rational mind, and Mary represents the heart center of our life. Joseph, as the rational mind, is incapable of planting the seed of divine love in the heart center which eventually brings the Christ, the divinity within, to birth. That divine seed can come only from the higher nature, from the love-wisdom center represented in the Bible as the overshadowing Spirit — which it is.

What do the shepherds represent — those who keep watch over their flocks by night? Now, your interpretation of the symbolism of these matters need not agree with mine. But, to me, the shepherds represent advanced individuals who are sufficiently awake to be aware of the reality of divine birth — of initiation — and sensitive enough to catch the angel song, not with the physical ear, but with the subjective or inner hearing.

According to Luke, the spoken word of the first angel to appear included this: "Be not afraid, for behold, I bring you good news of a great joy which will come to all the people." And the heavenly chorus sang: "Glory to God in the highest. Peace on earth, goodwill toward men." Are we awake? Do we listen to that heaven-sent song? We are shepherds, are we not? Or at least called to be such, keeping watch in prayer and meditation over the sleeping flocks (the unawakened ones) during the night of men's suffering. Ponder on that call, that task, that joyous privilege. Let us watch...and listen...and hear and respond. Let us take our journey to Bethlehem, the place of New Birth, of beginning again. Let us kneel in spirit before the glory of the divine life born among men, in the stable, within man's animal nature — a miracle indeed. We are told that higher Beings, symbolized by the angels, are present at every real initiation, and there is truly divine melody. Unless we are on the 'path', we do not listen and are dull of hearing, as Isaiah and Jesus both commented, and we fail to make our journey into the presence of the Christ. What about the star? I am not interested whether or not a new star appeared in the sky at that time. In reality, those who have witnessed initiation and have conscious memory of it affirm that at a certain point in the ceremony the star of initiation shines out over the heads of those being initiated. Here is the significance of the star of Bethlehem.

The three wise men, or Magi, reported by Matthew (but not by Luke) are, I believe, workers in white magic and probably adepts or very advanced disciples who are present at every initiation. We are told that at such a time three of them form a triangle of light around the new initiate, stepping down the tremendous energy to a more tolerable level. Perhaps these energies are symbolized by the gifts of the Magi: gold, frankincense and myrrh.

Gold is a most precious metal, symbolic of highest values. Alchemists work to transmute baser metals into gold. Truly, when we have undergone initiation, lesser values of life have been transmuted into the gold of higher character.

Frankincense represents true beauty — the aesthetic values and dimensions of life. It is when we have risen to the level of initiation that we are in possession of life's real incense.

Myrrh was used in ancient times to prepare bodies for burial. It represents pain, suffering and sorrow. Though this may come as a surprise to some, pain also is an important element in the life of the initiate. Far from being spared pain, as we advance in life, we come to experience it on a higher level — a sharing in the suffering of bruised humanity. This is a redemptive level of pain in which we all can share, and will do so increasingly. Myrrh cannot be left out of the gifts.

Finally, what about Herod who, according to Matthew, tried to destroy the newborn babe? As we ponder this question, we become aware that Herod represents the lower life, the lower desires. These, like Herod, are possessive of their power over us and are loath to give it up. Herod is told (and these lower forces become aware) that Christ is born to grow and to reign. But Herod will do all in his power to prevent this.

Who gives the needed protection to this new initiate, the babe in Christ, the 'little one' as the Bible calls the fledgling initiate? Here is where Joseph, the rational mind, comes in. This concrete mind cannot fertilize the heart center with the divine seed and cannot, like Mary, give birth. But the concrete mind does have its real value. Instructed from above, as Joseph was instructed by angels, it forms an important part of the holy family of our nature, providing protection from above for the new life. This might be called the protection of common sense, or practical good judgment. Thus the new life, born and growing in the heart center, is kept from 'going off the deep end', as we sometimes say, and being destroyed.

Also, do not forget Mary, the love of the heart. For the heart and head need to be always in harmony and co-operation in order for the new life within us to grow to maturity and truly reign in our life.

December 1982

1. See *The Gospel Story and the Path of Initiation* by Benjamin Creme in *Share International,* Vol. 1, No. 6, and in *Maitreya's Mission,* pp. 171-174.

8. The Choice Is Always Ours

More than two thousand years ago a fiery leader of ancient Israel spelled out multiple choices to his people. Then he gave them this challenge: "Choose you this day whom you will serve...But as for me and my house, we will serve the Lord." (Josh. 24:15) Joshua's concept of God may not have been as high or as universal as that which Jesus set forth and embodied in His day, nor as comprehensive as we are permitted to embrace today. But he was choosing in accordance with the best he knew. Just as importantly, he was offering his people a freedom of choice which was rare in his time.

Unfortunately such open freedom appears to be all too rare in our day also. The extreme governmental pressures for conformity applied to so many people in so many parts of the world now are appalling. These are demands to conform to the ideology and life style decreed as the only acceptable way of life. These cruel and inhuman measures seek to throttle the free spirit of man — to deprive him of his freedom of choice. But we need to ask: are such repressive systems but the harsh death throes of a slowly dying order? We need to get a complete picture of the world situation. And to do so we must shift our gaze to something more vital than the repressive measures being applied by so many governments and by some religious 'authorities'.

From some points of view, it is amazing and refreshing to see today how many people all around the world are refusing to knuckle under to any and every kind of repressive authority — no matter how great the cost. We may be inclined to wince a bit when we see how high the cost of free choice turns out to be in so many places — a price often exacted in terms of incarceration, torture, and even death. But if we can see all this in terms of man's invincible spirit — victorious, as the Bible puts it, over "sin and death" — we may be greatly encouraged.

In New Testament times we find the account, recorded in the book of Acts, of how the Sanhedrin (the high court in Jerusalem) decreed that the apostles or friends of Jesus would not be permitted to share the good news of Christ by speaking in His name. The response of those brave souls has been an inspiration to courageous and aspiring souls ever since. In the face of such repression they couched their reply in these unmistakable words: "As for us, we must obey God rather than men." How inspiring is the courage they embodied. Most followers of Christ like to be law-abiding citizens of whatever country they live in, and in most cases they truly are. But when conscience seems to require an act of civil disobedience, we have our charter for such an act in the New Testament.

Most of those disciples eventually paid with their lives for their high choices, and the fearless acts which followed. But all indications are that they did it in a spirit of love, of joy and of victory. Perhaps Paul expressed for all the apostles the true calibre of their dedication when he said: "Whatever gain I had I counted as loss for the sake of Christ. Indeed I count everything as loss because of the surpassing worth of knowing Christ Jesus my Lord. For his sake I have suffered the loss of all things and count them as refuse, in order that I may...be found in him... That I may know him and the power of his resurrection...Not that I have already attained this...But one thing I do, forgetting what lies behind and striving forward to what lies ahead, I press on toward the goal for the prize of the upward call of God in Christ. Let those of us who are mature be thus minded." (Phil. 3:7 ff)

Perhaps one reason I have been impelled to quote extensively from this letter which Paul wrote to the church he had founded at Philippi is that this letter was written in prison when Paul was facing possible execution for his brave stand for Christ. Even in such circumstances the choice for him was ever clear. Indeed in that same letter he wrote: "Even if I am to be poured out as a libation upon the sacrificial offering of your faith, I am glad and rejoice with you all. Likewise, you should be glad and rejoice with me."

It is great to get a lift from the courageous choices of men of the past, as well as brave souls today. But to bask in the reflection of their glory is not enough. The challenges must be faced directly by us today, both individually and collectively. Choose this day whom you will listen to and whom you will serve. Will we take the way of doubt and fear? Will we yield to the tempting nether voices which whisper: "Maybe it is not so. Maybe the Christ, Maitreya, is not present in a physical indestructible body. Maybe that is too much to expect. Perhaps we have to settle for less: for the old order of things under which we wanly hope for a better day and for some other form of release from the terror and starvation which stalks our world."

But we do not have to settle for that fear-inspired scenario. The choice still is ours. Dare we accept the strong assurances which Maitreya gives us and base our thoughts and lives on them? Let us attune ourselves to strong words such as these from Message No. 134:

"Try to believe, My friends, that I am here.

Try to accept that your Brother of Old is among you, and take up the challenge I give to you.

Help Me and help your brothers to make known My Presence.

Take the simple step of trust and awaken to your true worth.

Many await Me in fear, knowing not the cause of their confusion.

My friends, where fear stands, trust may not.

Why, then, hold to fear?

My Presence is apparent all around you.

Awaken to that fact.

Open your eyes to the changes in your world,
in your own heart, in the Light of Joy in your child's eye.

Know that I am with you in these ways,
My friends, and help save the world.

Your cries have been heard.

Your longings have reached My heart.

Your pain is Mine.

My Treasure shall I bestow on you."

What have we to lose but our fears and our chains, binding us to an outmoded past. Of course we may have to put up with the pity of well-meaning friends who fear we have 'gone off our rocker'; perhaps the scorn of the worldly-wise who may proclaim that we are deluded in listening to what they consider such drivel; or the blast of the so-called orthodox who pontificate about the anti-Christ.

But what a small price to pay in comparison to the fiery courage of a St. Paul or the sacrificial love of a Mother Teresa and countless others of our own day. Let us not forget that indeed the choice is always ours. May we joyously choose to be numbered with those who stand up and affirm: as for me and those who march with me under the banner of this New Day, we will serve the Lord in His way of sharing, of justice, of brotherhood, and of love. For we see no other way except that of chaos and destruction. And after all, what is that but anti-God, anti-Christ, and anti-humanity?

February 1983

9. The Five-fold Path to Resurrection

Our Western world has long thought of Easter as a symbol of nature rising out of its icy tomb of winter into its color pageant of spring; and of Jesus rising out of His borrowed tomb of death into His resurrection glory, thus bringing not only new hope but a new dimension of life to His disciples. And it is to be remembered that disciples of Christ may be members of any of the world's religions, or of none.

Let us then seek to discover the meaning of this Easter or Aries full moon festival for ourselves, as disciples or aspirants to discipleship, and for humanity, which has been called the world disciple. Alice A. Bailey, in *The Rays and the Initiations*, has reported for us, from the Tibetan, a rule for disciples and initiates which bids us: "Know — express — reveal — destroy — resurrect."

This five-fold admonition may seem shocking to us at first, indicating how many steps are necessary before we are ready for our complete resurrection. However (for our encouragement), there is another sense in which, if we are on the spiritual path, and are doing our part, we are in a continuing process of resurrection. That is, we are in the process *now* of either slowly or rapidly rising out of old habits and old prisons into greater light, love and spiritual power. Let us not forget this truth. Its realization is a needed companion on our journey. And that wondrous journey will be advanced once we come to understand and experience what is involved for us in the four key words: Know — express — reveal — destroy.

What does it mean to *know*? Fifty years ago, as a young denominational minister, I was involved in and struggling with many beliefs. I was trying desperately to hold on to these beliefs, and feeling very insecure about it all. For instance, I was clinging to the belief that God — an awesome Being up there and out there somewhere — loved me. Yet I wondered how He possibly could love me, for I felt so unworthy of any real love. In the midst of that tangle of belief and doubt there seemed little, if anything, that I could really know for sure.

Since then, through prayer and meditation, and continuing through faulty attempts to live a life of discipline, dedication and unselfish service, I am grateful that now I have arrived at a place of knowing, at least in some things. This level of consciousness, where we not only believe but know that we are beings of eternity, at one with God, is a precious achievement. Beliefs can be snatched from us either by logic or illusion, and often are. But what we really know cannot be taken from us by any means whatsoever. Such knowing emerges from our intuitive or buddhic level of being and, as DK indicates, eventually becomes "direct awareness of God."

When we have progressed to that level of true knowing, then we are in touch with the truth of Christ, which we become ready to express. Lacking this in the Piscean Age: "In the Christian Church, men have expressed themselves, not Christ; they have imposed their interpretations of truth on truth itself; they have created a massive organization in every land but a living organism is non-existent." (*Rays and Initiations*, p. 296)

But as disciples we eventually rise above such entrapments of the lower self. Now His truth becomes our truth. Now we become ready to express His Plan of sharing, of justice, of brotherhood and love. For now it has become not only His Plan but our own as well; a Plan for the whole of humanity, seeking to find expression through us and through His disciples around the world. Can we not see that the purpose is that the truth and the Plan — through us and His disciples everywhere — should find acceptance and expression among the masses, the members of the human family everywhere?

As disciples we become aware of the divine life in every blade of grass, every drop of water and every human being. Hitherto this innate glory of God in those blades of grass, those drops of water and in most human beings has been hidden. Now this shining glory becomes revealed in and through these and all other aspects of nature. As disciples, whether we have realized it or not, we become channels for the revelation of this divine reality.

Does this fact seem too overwhelming at first, too awesome? We had best get used to it. For if we were to turn back or slip from the spiritual path, we would be back on the level of revealing our littleness, and expressing our selfish desires, our fears, and perhaps our greed and lust. But whatever aberrations we may slip into, we, as disciples, cannot long escape our 'dharma' (spiritual duty) of revealing through our life and service the wisdom and the Plan of God. For it is, after all, the wisdom and Plan of our real Self, Monad, or divine Spirit. Down here in the personal scramble of life on the physical plane we may have evaded our true Selves for aeons of time, but as disciples we can do so no longer. For us that time of evasion is past. As someone has put it: "May the love and light that is in Christ stand revealed in us, that we may renew and increase our service to our fellow men."

In the past — a past which we may or may not remember, and of which we may now feel ashamed — we have no doubt been involved in destruction of a harmful kind. That is, a kind of destruction which dashes to bits the hopes, the dreams, the aspirations, and sometimes the lives of others; yes, and sometimes of ourselves. But the kind of destruction we are intended to be involved in now is different: namely, the destruction of barriers which separate and divide people on the basis of race, color, religion, age, sex, nationality or whatever. Such barriers sometimes carry the label of prejudice. But whatever their name or nature they must go! And truly they are in the process of being destroyed. Sometimes that destruction is not as rapid as we would like. But isn't that where we as disciples come in? As we rise to the level where we really know, express and reveal the oneness of all life, our part in the needful and beneficent process of destruction comes more and more into focus.

This participation in destroying the old and limiting walls of separation prepares us to become "willing builders of the shining temple of humanity." This is a radiant goal set for us by the Christ, in one of the Messages He has conveyed to us. How we long to fulfill our part in this glorious task.

The complete resurrection into full citizenship in the spiritual kingdom, or Kingdom of God, may lie far ahead for us. I know it does for me. For that consummation takes place at the fifth initiation. And that constitutes being raised to the position of a Master of the Wisdom in the Spiritual Hierarchy of our planet. But lesser resurrections take place along the way. Through these other steps, as we come to know, express, reveal, destroy and build, we are in the process of rising out of our self-made tombs of darkness and limitation into the light and glory of Easter morning.

Let us realize that we too can experience transforming resurrection, not only symbolically, but in our daily lives. Yes, we can, if we so choose and daily apply ourselves — in love, in trust, in joy, and through sharing on many levels.

April 1983

10. The Contribution of Religion in the New Age

As a backdrop for what I have to say about religion in the New Age, I would like to begin with a few words about religion in the old Piscean Age. First, it is important to remember that religion in this past age has helped many individuals, and I am one of those who has been a recipient of the benefits of this individualistic religion. The Piscean Age religion has produced many truly outstanding religious leaders, from Jesus and His disciples to, in our own time, Albert Schweitzer and Martin Luther King.

Too often, though, religion in the past has not operated on this high level. All too frequently it has been crystallized, dogmatic, and even condemnatory. Recall that Jesus once asked, "If your son asks for bread, would you give him a stone? And if he asks for fish, would you give him a scorpion?" Yet, sadly enough, that is what has sometimes happened in religion in the past. People have come hungry for the bread of life and have been given the stone of argumentation and disputation. They have come asking for the fish of wisdom and sometimes received the scorpion of damnation and threats of hell.

So as we stand in the dawn of this New Age, some are saying: "Religion — who needs it; away with it; let's have done with all that claptrap." And if religion really consisted of such claptrap, divisive and dogmatic authority, most of us here would undoubtedly join the chorus. But listen to the Master DK's definition of religion: "Religion is the invocative appeal of humanity and the evocative response of the Greater Life to that cry." To me, this means that religion in the New Age will be — and to some extent is already becoming — a vital, inner, subjective approach to the hidden divinity within — our true nature, plus an answering response from that light, love and power which is the One Life and within which we live and move and have our being.

The Tibetan Master DK also says that the typical prayer and worship of the past is to be replaced by the science of invocation and evocation in the religion of the New Age. The fact is that worship services — as we have called them in the past — have involved, first of all, the idea that we are trying to contact a God who is external to us — out there some place — and that the way to make this contact is by doing homage before him: "Let us worship and bow down; let us kneel before Jehovah our Maker." The idea behind that worship was that the way to induce the divine majesty to pay attention to us and save us was to placate His wrath and prostrate ourselves before him. If successful we might then prevail upon him to turn His face toward us, smile on us and set aside His stern laws to help us.

The psychological accompaniments and outer trappings supporting this idea included the typical formal church with its hard pews and kneeling places, with all the people facing in one direction toward the place of external authority — a high altar, a high pulpit. Thus the lowly worshipper had to look up to the berobed and decorated authority figure — priest, pastor, prelate or rabbi — expounding external authoritative teachings gleaned from the Bible, Pope or Torah, telling the poor sinners what they must believe and what they must not believe; what they must do and what they must not do; how they must dress and wear their hair and the like.

An extreme picture? Yes, in some cases it is a very extreme picture for, as I said earlier, religion at its best in the old age helped many people. But if you have heard stories like the one from my own part of the world, where a prelate in our enlightened Southern California denied communion to women who belonged to certain organizations stressing women's rights, you might think that the picture I have painted is not so extreme after all.

It should be clear now why the Tibetan says our outmoded worship and our authoritative dogmas need to be superseded by a new kind of gathering. A gathering to invoke light, love and divine will (power), thus evoking or calling forth from the divinity within and beyond us all the enlightenment, love-wisdom, and power-for-good that this world desperately needs, and for which we all hunger.

Thankfully, the first buds of this new springtime of religion are already to be seen in some places — places where religious groups are no longer calling their gatherings 'worship' but rather festivals and celebrations. I am grateful for the widespread celebration of the three linked festivals of Easter, Wesak and Humanity. And I am thankful for the monthly festivals at or near full moon times celebrated all over the world. Also, many such groups are no longer sitting in fixed straight rows looking at the back of all the people ahead of them, looking up, striving to catch inspiration from an authority figure high above them imposing his ideas on the weary audience.

Now we develop group leadership and we sit in circles more conducive to the flow of the group energies. We search within for the liberating truth, finding the strength and joy which send us forth in service to the Spiritual Hierarchy through service to our sisters and brothers — our fellow seekers. People sometimes ask how you can arrange very large groups in circles. Well, they knew how to do that in ancient Rome and they even know how to do that today in our modern sports stadiums.

So religion in the New Age, as it shakes off the chains of external authority, divisive doctrines and outmoded worship; as it learns the science of invocation and evocation; as it tunes in to the full moon opportunities in festivals throughout the year; as it increasingly develops group leadership and Soul consciousness; as it helps prepare the way for the reappearance of the Universal Christ; as it does all this, religion in the New Age will be making a contribution far greater than we can envision here and now.

The big question is: how many religions of today are open-minded enough, or can become flexible enough, to make this great change? How many will be left behind with a fossilized and dead shell of an old religion which is fit only for burial? Are you and I ready? Are we fully enough ready to be actually moving out of the old dead forms into the new vitality? Are we sowing the seeds of the New World Religion wherever we can? There is one who points out to us that when we sow good seed some will fall on the hard-beaten path where it has no chance at all, and some will fall on shallow soil or among thorns where weeds and thorns will grow up and choke off the new growth. But some seed will fall in good soil and bear fruit — thirty fold, some sixty fold and some even a hundred fold. So let us be at work sowing the seeds of the religion of the New Age.

Today a wonderful thought in this new dawn is being given if we can tune in to it, and the thought is this: that a secret Plan is hidden in our groups and in our group consciousness; that our groups are big in purpose, big in potential, big because of this Plan; and that God, who dwells within us and our groups, knows and progressively reveals this secret Plan of things He will do for the world using our group consciousness, our hands, our heads, and our hearts.

June 1983

11. Love: The Key to Sharing

"A new commandment I give to you, that you love one another; even as I have loved you, that you also love one another." This pronouncement, given through Jesus and recorded in John's gospel, seems a bit surprising at first. Why did he call it new? The command to love one's neighbor as oneself had been given long before, and recorded in the Old Testament. In the New Testament it has been elevated to prominence by Jesus, as He pronounced it to be equal to the command to love God with heart, soul, mind and strength.

The fact is that some degree of emphasis on love is found in all the great religions. Marcus Bach, director of the Fellowship for Spiritual Understanding, and a long-time teacher in the field of world religions, capsulizes such emphasis in his flier entitled *Love In The World's Great Religions*. It includes these quotes:

Christianity — Beloved, let us love one another, for love is of God.

Confucianism ---- To love all men is the greatest benevolence.

Hinduism ---- One can best worship the Lord through love.

Islam — Love is this, that thou shouldst count thyself very little, and God very great.

Sikhism — God will regenerate those in whose hearts there is love.

Judaism ---- Thou shalt love the Lord thy God with all thy heart, and thy neighbor as thyself.

Jainism ---- The days are of most profit to him who acts in love.

In what sense, then, is Jesus' commandment that we love one another even as He loves us a new commandment? The answer lies in the completeness and unconditional nature of this love of which He speaks, which He poured out to His disciples then, and which He continues to pour out even now ---- to the whole world.

Consider this: I may love my neighbor as myself. But if my love for myself is limited, sentimental and conditional, then my love for others can turn out to be also very limited, and thus of questionable value. But if I rise to the level where I love as Christ loves, from the higher Self or Soul level, then that is a new expression of love indeed, at least for most persons. This is the quality of love shown on the cross in the words: "Father, forgive them for they know not what they do." Such love flows from the buddhic or Christ-consciousness plane, with the power to lift me and all humanity out of our darkness and fear into the clear light of brotherhood and oneness.

But in what sense can such love be the key to sharing? The answer should be quite evident. For if our love is not of this high Soul quality, then whatever sharing we may do will be very limited in scope, tainted by fear, and lacking in the needed motivation. Selfish individuals and governments sometimes do a bit of sharing — often because they are in a situation where they think they cannot avoid it — and usually with the motive of getting something deemed important for themselves in return.

But a Mother Teresa or a Francis of Assisi pours out love so fully that it results in a sharing of life-energy, substance, and loving service with no strings attached, asking nothing in return. Can we do likewise? Yes, we can, when we rise to the level of our true Selves, and serve from that high plane. Then this buddhic quality of love, which gives freely, making no demands, will naturally pour forth from us with the kind of sharing on all levels, which not only has power to heal and uplift a shattered world, but which also immeasurably enriches and frees our own lives as well.

Long ago the Christ, speaking through Jesus, expressed this truth in many ways, including the following gem (which we seem so slow to comprehend): "Give, and it will be given to you; good measure, pressed down, shaken together, running over, will be put into your lap. For the measure you give will be the measure you get back." (Luke 6:38)

Likewise, in the Messages which the Christ has been giving us through Benjamin Creme since 1977, these twin factors of love and sharing have been shown to be the paired principles basic to all that He comes to do among men, and that these principles of love and sharing must be focal in our life and work as we let him work through us to implement His purpose. In Message No. 91, for instance, He states: "My Light embraces all. My Love fills their hearts." In that same Message He stresses: "Learn to share, to grasp your brother's hand and know him as yourself. Teach this simple Truth and you teach the Law of God." Let us note that with this realization of oneness the matter of sharing is seen in a new light — for we are in effect sharing with ourselves!

Many passages from these poignant Messages of the Christ might be cited to show how sharing flows naturally from real love. Let me conclude with a beautiful quote from Message No. 57. He bids us to send His words of love "...throughout the world and reach the hearts of your brothers. Help them, too, to share in a great manifestation of God's Love, and awaken them to the promise of the future...The central point of My Plan is to evoke in men the desire to share, for on this Principle all else rests. Sharing, My friends, is an attribute of God. To become the gods which you are, this Principle must govern your lives. Allow Me to remind you of this simple Truth once again and show you the path to the future. My Blessing goes with you all."

May we do our best to embody such fullness of outgoing love that true sharing will constitute our joyous outreach on all levels of our 'dharma' of service — service offered to Maitreya and to all our sisters and brothers everywhere.

July 1983

12. No Justice Without Sharing

Maitreya makes it clear, in His Messages, that there can be no peace without justice, and no justice without love and sharing. But in the long history of man the concept of justice has not always been thus equated with love.

The biblical assertion, "Vengeance is mine, I will repay, saith the Lord," is often quoted to portray justice as punishment, as retribution. This is a far cry from the concept of the justice of love. In the law attributed to Moses it is plainly stated: "When a man causes disfigurement in his neighbor, as he has done, it shall be done to him, fracture for fracture, eye for eye, tooth for tooth; as he has disfigured a man, he shall be disfigured." (Lev. 24:19-20) It may be surprising to note that this law of supposedly equal justice was set forth to curb the practice of exacting unlimited vengeance. In the fourth chapter of Genesis we read where a man named Lamech boasted to his wives: "I have slain a man for wounding me, a young man for striking me. If Cain is avenged seven fold, truly Lamech seventy-seven fold."

Sadly enough, this retributive concept of justice, "eye for eye and tooth for tooth," still prevails in too many parts of the world, and even in so-called courts of justice. Not only this, but even Lamech's concept of excessive retribution is still seen in cases, for instance, where a parent strikes, wounds, and some- times even disfigures or kills his child as punishment for minor infractions of parental law.

In fact, the thought-form of retribution as justice is so strongly ingrained in men's thinking that some theologians still are struggling with the question of how to reconcile divine justice with divine love. This quandary arises not only through a misconception of justice, but of love as well. For love is often thought to be sentimental weakness. Surely the more we study and meditate on the gospel — the good news — of Christ, both in Palestine long ago and in His Messages today, the more truly we will come to understand that love means justice, and justice is the way of love. In the Sermon on the Mount, as reported by Matthew, Christ says (speaking through Jesus): "You have heard that it was said, 'an eye for an eye, and a tooth for a tooth.' But I say to you...if any one strikes you on the right cheek, turn to him the other also... Love your enemies, and pray for those who persecute you, so that you may be sons of your Father...for he makes his sun rise on the evil and the good, and sends rain on the just and on the unjust." (from Matt. chapter 5) Here we can see not only that Jesus was correcting the mistaken thought-form about justice as retribution, but was revealing that love is a creative and surprising response to wrong.

This is spelled out even more fully in the present day Messages from Maitreya. In studying Messages 101 to 140 I discover that in at least 35 instances He is calling for justice, as the expression of love and sharing, and as a major prerequisite for peace. Just a few examples will make this clear: "I show men that the Path to Justice is simple... I speak of God's Truth, of the Light within mankind, of the need for trust, the Love of brother for brother... As you place your foot on the Path to Justice and Love so do you begin the ascent to God." (Message No. 108)

"Justice must and shall be done. The world groans for Justice. The true reason for man's problems today is the absence of Justice and Love... This gracious gift of Love and Just Sharing stems from God. Only through its correct manifestation can God be known. Teach men this, My friends, and you teach a great and simple Truth... I come to show you the simple Path to God through Love, to teach you the techniques of Love, the way forward through Love and Justice, correct relationship of man to man and thus to God." (Message No. 101)

"When you see Us you will know that the new Time, the New Age, has begun, the time of Sharing and Justice, of Love and Brotherhood, the time of the Law of God." (Message No. 136) "I need your help to come before you, to bless this world and teach, to show men that the way forward is simple, requires only the acceptance of Justice and Freedom, Sharing and Love." (Message No. 140)

Through these and other Messages it becomes plain that our share in the work involves not only embodying these principles of justice and love, of sharing and brotherhood within ourselves, but also the task of teaching these transforming truths to others. At times perhaps we feel a bit overwhelmed by this responsibility. But do we need to feel thus overwhelmed or overburdened? Why should we, when we have available the great help of the Christ and the Masters, as we gladly commit ourselves to this gracious opportunity for sharing?

By what means, then, are we intended to teach these truths? The answer, I would think, would include every means available to us. Can we not write letters to friends and editors, at least alerting them to the possibility of a way out of the present impasse? Can we not raise questions with some persons, not imposing anything on them, but asking them what they think of these truths? Thus we will be planting seeds which will bear fruit later on. And inwardly, through meditation, through transmission work, surely we can send out the energy of these principles, to be used by the Hierarchy in their wisdom, for the healing of men and nations. And, in addition to all this, perhaps we teach more effectively than we know by what we are, by what we think, and by living in the Christ spirit of light, of love, and wisdom. What do you think?

September 1983

13. Burning Away Barriers

Barriers often reside within our emotions and lower mental equipment — obstacles which tend to separate us from:
 a. Our own higher or divine Self;
 b. Our fellow human beings;
 c. The Spiritual Hierarchy — the Christ and the Masters.

One of the most active and troublesome of these barriers is fear. It spawns a whole brood of children: worry, anxiety, procrastination, blocked energy, misdirected action, undue tension, stomach ulcers, etc; and it often produces resentment, hostility and violence, both verbal and physical.

Throughout the Bible, as well as the present teachings of the Christ, we find oft-repeated warnings against yielding to fear and living in fear. In addition we are given ample clues to help us burn away this obstinate barrier. How? Through love and trust, through cultivating the realization of our oneness with everyone, and through sharing.

In Is. 43:1-3, for instance, we find this great assurance: "Fear not, for...you are mine. When you pass through the waters I will be with you, and through the rivers, they shall not overwhelm you. When you walk through fire you shall not be burned, and the flame shall not consume you. For I am your God...your Savior." This was written centuries before Jesus' time, but it could well have been written today. How graphically this passage describes the rivers of fear which swirl around us today. And the fires of opposition through which we are called upon to walk right now. Thus how real is the assurance of the divine promise: that the rivers shall not overwhelm us, and the flame shall not consume us. This assurance can be very strong if we accept the word: I will be with you. In the New Testament, and in Maitreya's Messages, that word is stated even more affirmatively in the present tense: "I am with you always." (Matt. 28:20 and Message No. 130)

In Luke 12:29-34 the Christ, speaking through Jesus, spells out very clearly this problem of fear and its solution: "Do not seek what you are to eat and what you are to drink, nor be of anxious mind. For all the nations of the world seek these things; and your Father knows that you need them. Instead, seek his kingdom, and these things shall be yours as well. Fear not, little flock, for it is your Father's good pleasure to give you the kingdom. Sell your possessions and give alms; provide yourselves with purses that do not grow old, with a treasure in the heaven that does not fail, where no thief approaches and no moth destroys. For where your treasure is, there will your heart be also."

The 'little flock' of those who hear and heed and seek to follow the Christ is much larger today. But small or large, we are assured we need not fear, for it is our Father's good pleasure (Plan) to give us the kingdom. He is of course speaking of the spiritual or fifth kingdom — in the process of being established right here in this physical realm. And He pointed out then, as He emphasizes today, that the key to the solution lies in sharing. Furthermore, then as now He indicates the kind of treasure, in the high spiritual levels of our being, which nothing can take from us, concluding: "Where your treasure is, there will your heart be also."

Over and over again, and in simple direct language, Maitreya makes plain to us that love and trust constitute the power which can burn away the barriers of fear and its allies. Or, to change the figure of speech, love and trust are the solvent which effectively melts away fear, worry, anxiety, and all such barriers to self-realization, and the realization of oneness with all.

Let us look briefly at a few more of the Christ's Messages given through Benjamin Creme; passages where the solution of the problem of fear and all that goes with it is sharing: "When you see Me, fear not ---- I come not to scold but to teach... Know that My Love is with you always. Know that My Shield protects you. Know that My Will upholds you. Know this, My friends, and fear not." (Message No. 136)

"I shall remove from your hearts the fear of death, the fear of life itself, the fear of your brother and of yourself... Many await My coming with some fear. Nothing but good shall grow where I tread. My Promise stands... I shall create among you a pool of Love from whose waters all may quench their thirst." (Message No. 123)

"Many await My coming with some trepidation, fearing the loss of all that they have loved, all that they have amassed and gained. Fear not, My friends, for the loss will be the loss of separation only, of division and fear, of envy and hate. To clear these from the world all must be remade. Know this, My friends, and be ready to share, to see your brother as yourself, to clasp him in your arms and call him friend. In this way, My brothers, you manifest God's Plan." (Message No. 125)

To conclude, let me acknowledge that in my own personal life I have known intimately this barrier of fear. I have struggled long and often fretfully with anxiety of many stripes and colors. But I also can bear witness to the validity of the solutions above indicated. For it is when I can forget myself and my petty 'needs', and rise — trusting in divine love and wisdom — that I find myself free of the old anxiety patterns, coming into the utter certainty of knowing truth, and experiencing the real joy of sharing.

October 1983

14. Release from Separatism and Pride

How often we hear remarks like: "I'm so proud of you," "I'm proud of my country," "You did us proud," and the like. Perhaps we do not realize how separative and dangerous such attitudes are, especially on the part of mature persons, and particularly for aspirants and disciples.

Let us concede that for developing personalities, such as children, pride may have a place. Indeed a sense of pride in accomplishment seems to play a part in the development of self-confidence — the building of self-esteem among youngsters. The eleven-year-old or the thirteen-year-old proudly exults in hitting a home run in baseball, or in being at the head of her/his class in school. Such expressions of pride do seem to have some value at these early levels of growth, and possibly among adults who have not reached emotional maturity.

How sad it is, however, when we as aspirants, and especially as disciples, seem not to have outgrown such juvenile and prideful habits. A wise writer warned us long ago that, "Pride goes before destruction, and a haughty spirit before a fall." (Proverbs 16:18) We may well ask, what is the nature of that destruction? On one level it may be mainly physical, as when an individual's proud boasting is experienced as a physical assault conveying the message: "I'll show you. Take this and this and this. Let this teach you a little humility." But on inner, subtle levels our pride brings destruction of a more serious nature. For it is an exact prescription for tearing down and eradicating our realization of universal brotherhood — our sense of oneness with all that is. What could be more destructive than that?

At first glance it might seem that pride and separativeness are twin enemies, set against us on our path to self realization (which is, of course, realization of oneness with all). But probably it would be more accurate to say that separativeness is the parent and pride the offspring. The Ageless Wisdom teachers confirm this, affirming that eventually we will see that separativeness is the only 'sin', in the sense that it gives birth to all the other wrongs which afflict humanity.

As the Master DK tells us through Alice A. Bailey: "If you were to ask me what, in reality, lies behind all disease, all frustrations, error and lack of divine expression in the three worlds, I would say that it is separativeness which produces the major difficulties." (*Esoteric Healing,* p. 82) On page 546 of the same treatise He says practically the same thing: "Evil, crime, and disease are the result of the great heresy of separateness." To quote a more recent pronouncement, we find Maitreya, speaking through Benjamin Creme, telling us: "The crime of separation, of division, of lawlessness must go from the world. All that hinders the manifestation of man's divinity must be driven from our planet. My Law will take the place of separation. My Law is the Law of Love, of Brotherhood, of Justice and Truth... My Law will succeed, for the Law of Love emerges from the Being of God, and thus cannot fail." And in Message No. 117 He admonishes us to do our part: "Remove forever the curse of separation, of loneliness and fear. Take heed, My friends, and do this, do this now."

It will become obvious to us, then, that when we overcome this 'heresy of separateness' we will be free from pride. For what basis could there possibly be for pride when we come to realize that we are at one with all that is? That each of us is one cell in the body of reality. A concomitant dividend accruing from overcoming separativeness is this: that we thereby free ourselves also from the converse side of pride — that which rears its ugly head in the form of feelings of inferiority, lack of self-esteem, and the like. This is the 'poor weak worm of the dust' idea which arises in some expressions of religion. Such feelings and ideas are no more possible than is pride when we realize the oneness of all. What a deliverance!

It behooves us, then, to pay heed to the wise teaching that the cultivation and expression of real love and wisdom provide us with the solution to our problems and the true fulfillment of our needs. The means to accomplish this release from feelings of pride as well as of inferiority — both of which tend to play hide and seek with us — are clearly spelled out for us in the teachings of the Spiritual Hierarchy. These teachings emphasize self-discipline, meditation (with study and contemplation on our own innate divinity), following the path of service, cultivating goodwill to all, and the practice of sharing, with love.

When we hold our focus on the realization that we are innately divine — one with God, one with Christ, and one with all — then we come to know that we can accomplish all this. To strengthen our assurance let us conclude with two more quotations from Maitreya: "I shall create among you a pool of Love from whose waters all may quench their thirst... I shall remove from your hearts the fear of death, the fear of life itself, the fear of your brother and yourself. I shall help you put behind you that ignorance, and to walk with Me in the new Light." (Message No. 123)

"My Plans shall not fail... My Will shall strengthen. My Teaching shall show you the nature of God... Take My hand, My friends, and let Me lead you over the river. Let Me guide you over the narrow bridge. Let Me show you the beauty which rests on the other side. That beauty, My friends, is your true Self. Help Me, My friends, to help you, and together let us transform the world." (Message No. 130)

November 1983

15. A Christmas Message
The Sword of Cleavage ---- Herod vs. Christ

In the gospel according to Matthew we read how king Herod sent his soldiers to Bethlehem in an attempt to find and destroy the infant Jesus (instrument of the Christ). Why did he try this dastardly deed? Because Herod had been told that the Christ was to be king. And that paranoid old monarch would tolerate no threat to his own selfish reign.

This of course is a parable or allegory of the battle which rages at some time, or times, within each human being. The 'Herod' of our lower nature organizes fierce battles against the developing Christ consciousness. For this personality nature — with its lusts, its fears, its rage and its pride — is afraid that the Christ power of love and wisdom is indeed destined to gain the upper hand in our life. Thus these dark aspects of our life will have to be banished or transformed, their 'turf' and their reign in our system handed over to the inner Christ. How threatened these old rulers become! For they have been in command so very long — through so many lives — that they will not easily give up our entrenched habits. They work up a storm of sound and fury. Or so I have found it to be in my life.

But when they do surrender to the light, love and joy of the Christ nature, what glorious transformation takes place! Lust is replaced by love; fear by trust; resentment by goodwill; and pride melts into joyous humility and confidence. Then, like the prodigal son, we know that 'we have come to ourselves' and are joyfully on our way home to the Father's House, the eternal Monad or Spirit within.

So let us give heed to this question: are our thoughts, utterances, and deeds at times giving aid and comfort to the old 'Herod' nature (which is sometimes called the 'shadow' or the 'Dweller on the Threshold')? Or are we succeeding in our effort to help the Christ power to take increasing control of all aspects of our nature?

Truly this is an urgent question. For the Christ has duly warned us: "He who is not with me is against me. And he who gathers not, scatters." (Matthew 12:30) What? Is there no neutral ground? Well, if there is, it is in the process of yielding rapidly either to Christ or Herod; to the Angel of the Presence or the fiendish old Dweller on the Threshold. Probably all of us who ponder on such thoughts as these would like to yield all to the Christ, if it just didn't take so much herculean effort. Why are our old habits of thought, words, and ways of behavior so stubborn? Why does it take such dedication and devotion and power of will to change them? Maybe it is because of their long entrenched rule. For so long they have reigned with such power. And, as we have been told so many times, 'power corrupts'.

An indication of such corruption may be found in some desire on our part, conscious or unconscious, to cling to the old selfish pleasures we know so well. Sometimes we want to take another fling at the old indulgences: like pleasure, prejudice, pride and personal power. Sometimes there is a hidden fear that when Christ takes control in us our treasures of tinsel and baubles — which still glitter like false gold — will be snatched from us. So we are afraid we will stand bereft of life's richness. How deeply glamored we have become in thus clinging to the old, empty treasure pouches of the past. Could we but see clearly, we would *know* that, when Christ rules in our lives, the tinsel will be transmuted into pure gold; the turbulent emotions of fear and rage transformed into serenity and bliss; and the proud towers of separative thought converted into the true citadel for the expression of the ruling Spirit or Monad. What a transformation, what joy, what victory! Truly it awaits us all *when we are ready for it.*

How then do we strengthen the forces of Christ within us — and induce the old negative powers to yield? Since we are approaching the mystic season of Christmas, let us look at some of the symbols connected with this new birth. For they can have deep meaning within us for our transformation. Some of these characters and events are related to us in the gospel according to Luke, others in Matthew. They have esoteric meaning for us when we learn to look at them as aspects of an important drama unfolding within us.

Let us think of Joseph as representing our concrete mind; Mary as a symbol of our heart center — where the New Birth or first initiation is said to take place. We can think of the watching shepherds as disciples who are awake to the heavenly music or angel songs within. And the Magi as Great Beings who always are present to help usher into our lives the Christ life and power.

In our inner pilgrimage from the reign of Herod to that of Christ, let us proceed without delay to our Bethlehem. We are not to think it beneath our dignity to enter the stable of the domestic animals, and thus make provision for the Christ consciousness to be born in the lowly level of our physical or animal nature. Are we ready to listen to those awakened disciples who hear and heed the angel song of peace, of goodwill, and the good news of sharing? If so, we can welcome the three kings or Magi, the three aspects of our inner divinity — light, love and will or power, the sovereigns of our own being which follow the Christmas star of initiation or New Birth which shines out above us as soon as we are ready. Let us gladly accept their proffered gifts of gold, frankincense and myrrh — not for our little selves, but as treasures to pour out in sharing with the needy world. Then we need to let Joseph, the rational mind, transport us far from Herod's jealous reach to the Egypt of life's inner mysteries; where the Christ life in us can grow to full maturity — as St. Paul puts it: "unto the measure of the stature of the fullness of Christ."

Thus, when we dwell in the Christ consciousness, His love and wisdom will be able to find expression through us. In this crucial hour of humanity's need, let us renew our dedication to the divine Plan. Then through creative meditation, right speech, wise action and true sharing we can do our part. In this way we may stand assured that the 'ounces of our weight' and the power of our love will really assist in banishing the Herods of our day (and of our own lives). Thus we can really count, by helping to bring in the reign of Christ — the way of love, justice, and sharing — to include all our sisters and brothers on this spaceship earth. Let us rejoice, and let the angel chorus resound within us.

December 1983

16. Our Voyage on the Sea of Life

Our life experience here in the flesh is portrayed in beautiful symbolic form in the fourth chapter of the gospel according to Mark. There, as well as in Matthew and Luke, we have the account of Jesus and His apostles in a ship or boat, crossing the Sea of Galilee. It is reported that such a fierce storm arose that the boat was rapidly filling with water, and the disciples were afraid they were going to sink. At that critical point they woke their sleeping Master, calling insistently for His help. By the power of His word He stilled the storm on the waters, and also calmed the fears of the disciples. Then He questioned them: "Why are you so fearful? How is it that you have no faith?"

Bible scholars on the exoteric level of investigation hold conflicting views about this biblical narrative. Some explain it away as a natural happening. They say that such storms on that body of water arise very quickly, and subside as suddenly. Fundamentalists, on the other hand, insist that Christ used supernatural or magical powers to still the storm.

But esoteric students of the Bible, such as Geoffrey Hodson (see *The Hidden Wisdom of the Holy Bible*, Vol. I) help us to see the hidden meaning of this and other biblical allegories and dramas unfolding in our own lives. Hodson suggests four keys for understanding this and many Bible passages. The first key: interpret such passages as dramas within us. Second, see that each character in the drama represents some level of our consciousness. Third, look for progress from one level of consciousness to another (e.g., the ancient Hebrews leaving slavery in Egypt, wandering in the wilderness, and later crossing the Jordan river and entering the promised land — progress indeed). The fourth key: many words in sacred literature have specific symbolic meanings; for instance, mountains signify high levels of consciousness.

If we will use these keys, very many passages in the Bible will have new and greatly enhanced meanings for us. Let us apply some of these keys to the account of the storm on the Sea of Galilee. Let the boat represent the outer vehicle in which we, incarnate in physical form, are taking our voyage across life's sea. We can readily perceive that the sea symbolizes our emotions, where fierce storms so easily arise. Consider the disciples as portraying many levels of our consciousness. We could have a field day considering the Simon Peter aspect within us, and that of John, the beloved disciple, and others. But what about Judas? Is he also there somewhere within us?

The most important voyager on our ship of life is, of course, the Christ. But why are we so hesitant to call to him for help? Why do we wait until such a severe storm or crisis arises? Is it because we are so insistent that we can 'make a go of it' on our own personality resources? So it seems to be. But when the crises we face get serious enough, then — provided we have had some Soul contact with the Christ consciousness — we may turn in desperation, like the disciples of old, to that higher Power.

When we earnestly call to him with all our being He never fails to come to our assistance. And He never fails to come to the assistance of humanity when the call is insistently and persistently made. Today it is evident that humanity has voiced that call. Some have done it consciously, loud and clear; others somewhat unconsciously. But the fact that the call has been made, with strength and persistence, makes it possible for this great Being to be in our world now, in an indestructible body, so constructed as to last him all through the Aquarian Age now dawning. Thankfully, He is here to help us banish our fears and hostilities and pilot our space-ship earth across the present troubled waters — and then across the calmer waters of Aquarius.

Indeed, He has assured us that He has heard our widely-voiced plea for assistance, and is here in response to our cry for help. Let us listen to His words, which come to us through the loving service of Benjamin Creme, who has permitted himself to be overshadowed by the Christ, and thus has become the channel for 140 of His Messages.

"Many there are throughout the world who call Me, beg for My return. I answer their pleas. Many more are hungry and perish needlessly, for want of the food which lies rotting in the storehouses of the world. Many need My help in other ways: as Teacher, Protector, as Friend and Guide. It is as all of these I come. To lead men, if they will accept Me, into the New Time, the New Country, the glorious future which awaits humanity in this coming age. For all this I come. I come, too, to show you the Way to God, back to your Source; to show you that the Way to God is a simple path which all men can tread; to lead you upwards into the Light of that New Truth which is the Revelation that I bring. For all of this I come. Let Me take you by the hand and lead you into that beckoning Country, to show you the marvels, the glories of God, which are yours to behold." (From Message No. 2)

Let us rejoice in gratitude for His great sacrifice in responding to our call. He has repeatedly made it clear that He is calling to us to respond on every level to His voiced need for our cooperation and assistance in the great Plan of God which unfolds before us — the divine Plan of love, of sharing, of justice, and brotherhood for all. So let us give ourselves unstintingly in service.

Then under His banner, in willing service to the Plan, we will find our fears giving way to glad assurance and life's voyage becoming ever more beautiful, with new hope and deep fulfillment for all — even those who have mistakenly been called 'the least, the last, the lost'.

February 1984

17. Aquarian Age Good Samaritan

One of Jesus' best known and most loved parables has given rise to an oft-quoted phrase common in everyday speech: the reference is to this or that 'good Samaritan' who has tried, sometimes with success, to give help to some stranger in need. The poignant story from which the expression is drawn was Jesus' response to a question from a lawyer who simply asked, "Who is my neighbor?"

Jesus replied that a man, going down from Jerusalem to Jericho, fell among robbers who stripped and beat him, leaving him by the roadside half dead. Note the symbolism as it applies to us. Is it not when we are descending from our holy city (Jerusalem) to the lower planes of experience that we fall among the thieves of our lower desires, and separative, prideful thoughts? Have we not all experienced how these felons strip, rob and beat us, leaving us gasping beside life's highway — sometimes even more than half dead, as far as our true life is concerned?

Next Jesus notes that two religious leaders came along that same road, first a priest and then a Levite or assistant minister. But both passed by on the other side of the road. Let us inquire within ourselves: is there a religious or pious aspect of our personality which is too busy or too 'holy' to look into the wounded aspects of our condition and provide resuscitation? Sadly I perceive that in my own life this has too often been the case.

Now, however, comes the part of the story where that which has fallen is raised up. A Samaritan (these were the despised and outcast people at that time) discovered the wounded man. He had compassion on him, administering oil and wine, the best first aid treatment then available. Then the Samaritan set him on his own beast of burden, and took him to an inn — which also served as hospital. There he personally took care of him. He also made a down payment on the hospital bill and promised to pay the balance, whatever it might amount to, "when I come again."

The account concludes with Jesus inquiring of the lawyer which of the three — priest, Levite, or Samaritan — proved neighbor to the man who fell among robbers. This learned and privileged man of the law apparently could not quite bring himself to say those two words, 'the Samaritan'. But even with his reluctance he had to acknowledge "the one who showed mercy on him." Don't you love the closing words of Jesus? For, without pronouncing any direct word of rebuke, He simply bids the man: "Go and do thou likewise." What a lesson!

Now it should not be difficult for us to identify the one who proves to be the good Samaritan in our lives: namely, the Christ consciousness of love-wisdom — not only coming to birth in our heart center, but growing step by step into maturity, thus coming into control of our personality. This inner power lifts us up from our wounded and broken condition. He, as our higher Self, ministers to us in countless ways, bringing restoration, healing and wholeness. How could we possibly make it without His oil for healing, and the wine of the intuition which this higher Self provides?

Now, as we are entering the Aquarian Age, let us inquire how this symbolic truth may apply to all humanity. Doubtless we are aware of how severely mankind has been beaten, robbed, stripped and pillaged by the marauders on life's Jericho road. Indeed our civilization has been left in a dying state by the selfish, separative interests too long left in control of the world's resources. And we religionists, the priests and Levites of today, sometimes have been too preoccupied with our own sectarian religious 'duties'. Thus, all too often, we have looked the other way, and passed by on the far side of the road.

But thank heaven the Christ has heard the cries of earth's suffering children, the many agonized cries for help rising from all parts of the globe. And He has responded. He comes *now* at this crucial hour of the world's need. He comes to administer His precious 'oil and wine' in the form of shared bread for the starving millions, and to lift humanity out of its broken and fragmented condition. Yes, and to bring us to that inn of light and love and joy where there is nurture and healing for all.

Let us recognize him as man's true 'Samaritan' for this New Age; the Water Carrier for this thirsty world, bringing the Water of Life to all who will receive it. But we must heed His urgent call to us, for our help and co-operation. As He holds up before us the shining example of the compassionate Samaritan neighbor, can we not hear His clear call to us: "Go and do thou likewise."

We must embody His way of love for all. We must take His way of sharing, the Samaritan's way of the good neighbor. We must add our weight, however small it may seem, to the lifting of the heavy load of our brothers' need. Does this task seem too great? The burden too heavy? Let us remember that we march under His banner and in His strength of love, sharing, justice and brotherhood. He blazes the trail, He leads the way, He imparts to us His strength and wisdom. Let us know that in him we cannot fail. We have His promise of victory, a promise that is valid through all time, and for eternity as well. Listen! Is He not saying with love to all of us: "Go and do thou likewise"? And He trusts us not to fail him and our sisters and brothers in need.

March 1984

18. Planetary Resurrection

Easter. What beautiful pictures it paints in our minds — what tremendous significance it has for us. Christian churches traditionally celebrate Easter in terms of Jesus' rising from the stone-sealed tomb of death to resurrection glory, victorious, as usually affirmed, over both 'sin' and death.

But many people now are resurrecting the significance of Easter from the tomes of ancient and medieval theology, and applying the symbolism to individual lives today. We picture ourselves rising from the dark, dark caves of doubt, guilt, and fear which we have fashioned for ourselves and inhabited for so very long. And truly, by letting the angel of our higher nature roll away the massive grave-stones which have blocked our way for ages, we can indeed step forth into the glorious sunlight (Soul light) of our real Self — resurrection indeed!

Let us inquire: is it not time for the human race — the world disciple — to emerge from the dark tombs and dungeons of the past? As it seeks to do so, however, it seems that there is not just one stone, but several boulders, blocking the way. Let us consider briefly three of the heaviest of these: namely materialism, nationalism, and sectarian religion.

The Tibetan teacher DK assures us that our age-long love affair with the kinds of things we can see, weigh, and hoard has reached the zenith of its glamorous power over humanity, and perhaps has even passed that point a bit. Yet when we consider the vast inequities and inequalities existing in our world today, with some rolling in 'the fat of the land' and wasting earth's abundance, while so many millions are starving, we get the impression that this stone of materialism still rests too heavily at the door of our self-made tombs.

There was a time in human history when emerging nationalism constituted a boon for man — a definite step forward. That was the period when regional, tribal units and small city-states were uniting to form nations. At least in many cases these nations provided multiple advantages in the erasing of trade barriers and the bringing of numerous benefits. 'In union there is strength' was the motto of individual states in America and elsewhere, coming together to form nations.

But the benefits of one age so often become the burdens of a later time. Today humanity has progressed so far toward the realization of its oneness that national boundaries and other barriers between nations present fearsome obstacles to international commerce and co-operation in so many fields. The solution, of course, lies not in the breaking up of nations into smaller units, but rather in the melting down of some of the barriers between nations.

If our eyes are open we can see that there has already been significant movement in this direction. Such associations as the European Common Market and other international trade agreements hold some promise. But the United Nations is perhaps the most important international development ever. We think of it in terms of its political aspects. But of course it has great impact also on educational, economic, social, and cultural levels. Though less than 40 years old the UN has accomplished, and continues to accomplish, so much more than most of us realize. It has been called 'the last best hope of mankind'. Perhaps it would be more accurate to describe it as the best plan to emerge to date. But, since it is still in its infancy, the UN at its present state of development is not the best we can hope for as we move forward. At the very least, however, the heavy stone of nationalism at the door of humanity's tomb is beginning to crack, letting some resurrection light stream through.

In something of the same manner that nationalism proved of definite value in the past, so also did separate religions. We are told, though I never counted them, that in the United States alone we have over 200 Christian sects or denominations, a few of them large, but many so small that they are little noted. Often these divisions are deplored, and perhaps rightly so. But, on the positive side, this opportunity to form new sects at will has served the cause of religious freedom. For example, when blacks in the mostly white Methodist church were treated as second-class citizens, and segregated to balcony seats apart from the main body of worshippers, they exercised their freedom to depart and form their own Methodist sects, such as the African Methodist Episcopal Church and others.

But in the present century the need for a different kind of freedom in religion has surfaced. Not the privilege of separating, but the freedom to unite across denominational lines, sometimes in spite of theological differences. This has produced local, regional, state, national, and world councils of churches, as well as conferences of Christians and Jews, etc. This movement toward union has provided many opportunities for co-operation: in relief work, social activities, and even at times in united worship services.

So this heavy stone of divisive religions, blocking humanity's progress, is also beginning to show some cracks, letting in a little of the light of universalism. This is to eventuate in the New World Religion, as the Tibetan calls it, of the Aquarian Age.

How grateful we should be that the Christ is now present with us: not only as a growing power within our hearts; not only as an overshadowing presence in the work of some disciples; but also in indestructible physical presence. Waiting in the wings, as has so well been said; ready for mankind's invitation to present himself world-wide with the Plan — God's Plan — which can roll away or smash to 'smithereens' all obstructing barriers to light, love, and abundant life for all the people of earth. And we must remember that as humanity rises out of its tomb into Easter light and life, that also serves to lift up the lower kingdoms of nature on animal, plant and mineral levels. Thus is planetary resurrection initiated.

This great Being reminds us over and over, however, that He is only the architect of the Plan, and that we must be the willing builders. That being so, let us re-dedicate ourselves, heart and Soul, mind and strength, to that Plan. Let us identify ourselves more with Soul than with little self; more with Spirit than with form, so that Soul-level service, unselfish sharing, divine love may flow through us and all seekers in the light; flowing out to all our sisters and brothers who have been groping in dire need and darkness. Let us never forget that the part you and I play in this planetary resurrection is vitally important. Thus let us give ourselves gladly and unstintingly to the divine Plan.

April 1984

19. Inner Mysteries Revealed

Those whose intuitive powers are awakened discover a wealth of symbolic meanings in Jesus' parables and other teachings. These secrets constitute spiritual riches not even surmised by those who see only the literal words. In one of these intriguing word pictures we find Jesus explaining why these deep treasures are available to His accepted disciples — while they remain hidden from the curious crowds of people who come seeking phenomena or miracles.

He explains to these chosen disciples that He is not showing favoritism, as a surface reading might suggest. He tells them it is because they have *seeing* eyes and *hearing* ears, while others, with their infatuation with phenomena — with things — really have closed their eyes and ears. That is, their deeper understanding is blocked out. A key statement on this is found in Matthew 13:16: "Blessed are your eyes for they see, and your ears for they hear."

It might be well to ask ourselves: can Maitreya, the Christ, truly say that of us today? Doesn't the answer depend on how deeply committed we are to Him? And how fully we give ourselves to His way of love and sharing? The disciples of old, to whom He revealed these secret truths, were people who had left everything else to follow Him and serve His cause. Is that the only way you and I can really have the seeing eye and hearing ear for understanding the mysteries?

The teaching under consideration is usually called 'the parable of the sower and the seeds' (found in Matthew 13). In it Christ shows how realistic He is, for He reveals that some of the good seed He sows falls on the hard path, by the wayside, where the birds come and gobble it up and other seed falls on rocky soil, where it has not much root and soon withers away. Still other seed falls among thorns, which choke off its growth.

Let us consider: do we get discouraged when we see this happening in the work we do? If so, let us listen to His further words: "Other seeds fell on good soil and brought forth grain, some a hundredfold, some sixty, some thirty. He who has ears, let him hear."

As we consider these widely differing results when the good seed is sown, it would be easy to put the burden on all those other folks, those who do not follow the route that we take, sometimes with such pride! It is so easy to see others as hardened, shallow, or choked with material attachments. But perhaps it is more fruitful to ask ourselves: is there still some hardened or crystallized place in our consciousness, where *we* may not be letting His truth penetrate? Second, is there still some shallowness in us, where the divine growth gets withered away for lack of rootage? Or third, do the thorns, which He described as "the worries of this world and the lure of riches," threaten to choke His word of love and sharing in us, "so it produces nothing?"

If we find any such problems blocking our way, let us inquire: how ready are we to yield fully the direction of our thoughts, words and actions to this great one, Maitreya? Surely we know that when He really has full sway in us, He removes the barriers so that our lives come to represent the good soil, bringing forth a harvest of a hundredfold, or at least sixty or thirty. (My farm background suggests that even that lowest level would represent a pretty good return on our investment with Him).

But when we invest life fully with Him we are not so much concerned with the level of the harvest. Nonetheless, we can indeed rejoice when our eyes and ears become truly open. For then, amazingly, the inner mysteries become revealed. And we rejoice as Souls to serve His cause of love, sharing, justice and brotherhood. Thus do we become junior partners with Him in meeting our brother's needs (along with our own). And thus do we help to usher in the mysteries of the dawning Aquarian Age.

May 1984

20. When the Walls Come Tumbling Down

A well-known Negro spiritual has this ingenious refrain: "Joshua fi't the battle of Jericho, and the walls came a tumblin' down." The biblical narrative behind this dramatic affirmation is found in Joshua, chapter 6. There it is reported that Joshua and his people, the ancient Hebrews, besieged the walled enemy city of Jericho ---- but not in the way we would expect.

First, Joshua had his army march once around the city each day for six days, with seven priests blowing their seven trumpets of rams' horns. Then on the seventh day this procedure was repeated seven times. At the climax of this complex ritual, all the people on command gave a triumphant shout of victory, and "the walls fell down flat."

What is the secret of all this? Is it the power of the number seven (so significant throughout the Bible) multiplied sevenfold? Is it the power of unified sound — with the trumpets blowing and all the people shouting in unison? Is it the power of affirmed faith? Note that while the walls were still standing Joshua commanded: "Shout, for the Lord has given [not will give — HRC] you the city." Is it a combination of all these factors? One final question: is all this a symbolic statement, not intended to be taken literally as an actual happening on the physical level?

In any case I see this allegory as having a direct application to our world in this, our day. Consider the many dividing walls which need to 'come a tumblin' down', so that humanity may be united in love and brotherhood:
- The glaring wall of missiles, tanks and bombs which separate East and West.
- The walls of national greed and short-sightedness that divide North from South.

- The barriers of selfishness which — even within nations — stand between rich and poor.
- The ancient walls of bigotry blocking the way to union between Eastern and Western religions.
- The walls of lust and chauvinism between male and female.
- The barriers of tradition, prejudice and fear between social castes and classes.
- The walls of pride and ignorance erected between the aspirant and the common man.

The question we must face is this: what in the world will cause these walls to "fall down flat"? We must know that nothing in the world will accomplish this, short of the divine Plan, to be worked out by us in putting into practice the Hierarchy's blueprint of love and sharing, justice and brotherhood. Do we honestly believe that this will accomplish the herculean task before us?

It appears to me that we had better believe it, understand it, and work at it with all our resources, for there is no other alternative. Let us searchingly ask ourselves: are we intended to be among the heralds of this Plan — to issue a clear trumpet note that all may hear? And dare we share in the 'shout' of victory, even while the tottering dividing walls are, nonetheless, still standing? We are told that when "Joshua fi't the battle of Jericho and the walls came tumblin' down," there was unified action, the expression of unity of purpose. Can we, the aspirants and disciples of the world, achieve such unity of purpose and such united action? The answer, my fellow pilgrims, lies within us — and the tremendous resources of faith and love which are at our disposal.

June 1984

21. A Time of Accounting

The word pictures which Jesus set forth to illumine the lessons He was teaching seem to be almost unequalled in their power to drive home a deep spiritual truth — through the telling of a simple story. These parables often appear in somewhat varied form in the different gospel accounts. This should not surprise us, since the narratives were handed down orally for many years before they were put into written accounts.

Take, for instance, the parable of the master and the talents (or pounds) distributed to the servants. We find this set out in the 25th chapter of Matthew and the 19th chapter of Luke. Matthew tells of a man going on a journey, delivering five talents to one servant, two to a second, and one to the third. "Now after a long time the master of those servants came and settled accounts with them." In Luke's account the master is said to be a nobleman going into a far country to receive kingly power. Here we find the nobleman delivering one pound each to ten servants. We might speculate that Luke put it this way because he was very democratic and so could not go along with the unequal distribution reported by Matthew. However, in spite of these differences, in both accounts the 'punch line' or main thrust of the story is essentially the same. Both agree that upon the master's or nobleman's return he requires an accounting. The first and second servants to report have made excellent use of the talents or pounds given them and thus have large returns to present. They are highly commended by their master. In Luke's version they are given much greater responsibilities — put in charge of several cities. According to Matthew they "enter into the joy of their Lord."

But the unprofitable third servant tells a sad story. Noting that his master was severe in his requirements, he had yielded to the glamor of fear. He had hid his lord's money — buried it in the ground according to Matthew's rendering — and came trembling to hand it back with no increase. The climax of the parable, when couched in personal terms, seems harsh indeed. For this worthless servant, as Matthew calls him, has his talent taken from him and he is cast into outer darkness. But when we view this story in the light of the Ageless Wisdom, perhaps we can see that it illumines an important truth. For when we put to wise and unselfish service the talents at our disposal (though we are not to be working for reward), reward comes as a by-product of our service. In Luke's view we are given greater responsibility (put in charge of ten cities or five). Of course if we were afraid of responsibility this would be a dubious reward. But in the life of those who serve thus from a Soul level such fear has been pretty well surmounted. And, as in Matthew's account, we do enter into the joy of our Lord.

On the other hand, if we yield to the glamor of fear — hiding our talent in the ground (the physical dimension) — we discover it has withered away. Thus we find ourselves indeed in outer darkness: "There men will weep and gnash their teeth." (Matt. 25:30) This parable is so very timely right now. For we are told that after Maitreya worked with and through Jesus 2,000 years ago, He did depart to a far country, the Himalayas, there to dwell in His light body. "Now after a long time," (Matt. 25:19) He has returned. And in many of the Messages He has given us through Benjamin Creme it is very evident that He is calling us to account. Look at His challenge given in Message No. 50: "Take Me to your hearts as I, My dear brothers and sisters, have taken you to Mine, and, working together, let us remake the world. Let us change all that is corrupt and useless in your structures, all that prevents the manifestation of your Divinity. Let us together show the way for the Little Ones and hold fast the world for them. I appeal to you to aid Me in My Task of succour. Help Me to help the world, and fulfill this life."

Again in Message No. 97: "Join My Army, My friends and brothers, and cleanse the world of hate. Sharpen the Sword of Love, My brothers, close your ranks around Me, and valiantly together into the future let us march." Thus this 'now' is a time of accounting — not only for our stewardship up to the present, but also a strong challenge to render a worthy accounting of the kind of service we are willing to offer now.

How can we hold back from His appeal to us in this passage: "My arms are held towards you My friends, asking for your trust, appealing for your help in remaking the world. Many are the tasks which lie ahead, many are the blows which must be struck for Freedom and Truth. I need all those in whom that truth shines to follow Me and help Me in My work." (Message No. 26) Can we escape His burning word as found in Message No. 27: "Those among you who wish to serve the world have placed before them now the opportunity of all lives. May you seize it, use it to the full, and create for yourselves and your brothers a new life." Truly let us unite in seizing this culminating opportunity of all the lives we have lived, that we may share in creating for ourselves and our brothers and sisters a new life. Thus, incidentally, we will be entering into the joy of our Lord, in Matthew's term. Or, as Maitreya puts it in Message No. 104: "Triumphantly teach and know the joy of Service. My Love goes with you all."

August 1984

22. "I Come in Time"

We have not only this strong assurance, "I come in time," (Message No. 120) but many other voiced pledges from the Christ that the Day of Declaration is assured, and that the victory of love and justice is certain. Furthermore, if we tune in to the place of knowing within ourselves, we realize, beyond all the doubts we may have entertained, that this is the unshakable truth. So why be worried about the date of His coming worldwide expression of Pentecost? Or about anything else, for that matter?

In New Testament times the thought of the leaders of Judaism, and many of the people as well, was so crystallized that the truth embodied and proclaimed by the Christ could not get through the hard shell of their preconceived ideas about the coming Messiah. It had been prophesied that Elijah would come first to prepare the way. And indeed he did, reincarnated as John the Baptist. But he was not recognized. It had been prophesied that the Messiah would come as a prince, a king of David's line. That was also fulfilled, but in an unexpected way.

For His was a spiritual reign, as He said: "My kingdom is not of this world." (John 18:36) Again, the crystallized expectation was for a Messiah, wielding political and military power, to drive out the hated Romans and restore the kingdom to Israel. They were far from ready to accept a Messiah who came as a peasant carpenter and homeless preacher, who eventually was nailed to a cross by soldiers of that Roman empire they expected him to destroy.

Now, since it is typical for the 'establishment' of any religion to become crystallized in time, perhaps it is not so surprising that the priests, rabbis, and pharisees could not recognize him, for they were gazing through the thick and astigmatic lenses of their own privileges, prejudices and panic.

But how about His own disciples? They had spent years hiking with Him and hearing His teachings. They had become teachers and healers through His example and spirit. They had shared to some degree in His Gethsemane and crucifixion agony. And they had become witnesses to Him in His resurrected body. Surely, we surmise, they at least should be free of such mistaken and crystallized thinking. But look at the question they asked Him during one of those resurrection appearances: "Lord, will you at this time restore the kingdom to Israel?" (Acts 1:6). This illustrates how very hard it is to break free of the thick shells of our old thought-forms. Those disciples seemed to be totally unaware that their thought was so crystallized.

Can we take an honest look at our own thought-forms? We wouldn't be guilty of anything such as those disciples of old engaged in, now would we? Yet if our anxious expectation becomes glued or riveted to the idea that the great Day of Declaration must come about now — or at least within the next few weeks or months — let us beware of crystallization.

If we will but honestly look and listen to the Christ, He will open our eyes and understanding to the fact that right now, without waiting, He is presenting us with our great opportunity to help, to serve. As He challenges us in Message No. 121: "I place before you now the opportunity to work for Me... Fashion a network of hope which will sustain the world." Are we rising to that opportunity with all our energy? That network of hope will not only sustain the world, but ourselves as well, will it not? Maybe it will help us get over our depressing worries about how soon that Day of Declaration will come!

Again and again He asks us why we should wait. For instance, in Message No. 109 He asks: "Why wait for the sight of Me to act, when from yourselves in trust you can perform much? Take a little in trust, My friends, and act today as the warriors of old, waiting not for confirmation but glad to be in the vanguard. I, Maitreya, pledge My word — all shall be well;

all manner of things shall be well. Therefore, My friends, fear not. Uphold the Light in men's hearts, the hope and trust in the future, and bring them to Me."

A clear emphasis on our contribution is given in Message No. 114: "All that I shall do, I shall do through you. Know this to be true, My friends, and work for Me... Make known where you stand, My friends, and relieve the lot of your brothers." He points out to us that to the degree that we work now for justice and brotherhood, and embrace both the principle and practice of sharing, we are fulfilling our mission for Him and for all our sisters and brothers around the world.

Let us read and re-read often His assuring Messages, that we may absorb and embody His love and some of His power as we give ourselves now to the great work to which He is calling us all. We remember that on the Soul plane we are already one. Let us also be united in our consciousness. Thus with singing joy we may work together in love, in sharing, in the furthering of justice and brotherhood, with the deep assurance that Maitreya is with us and in us; that He does indeed come in time — His time. And that His cause — the lifting and salvaging of the world — cannot fail.

September 1984

23. The Miracle of the Mustard Seed

How big is your faith? In reality can faith be measured by size, or only by quality, vitality? Jesus must have startled His hearers — all people of limited faith — when He declared to them: "Truly I say to you, if you have faith as a grain of mustard seed, you shall say to this mountain, 'Move hence to yonder place' and it will move, and nothing will be impossible to you." (Matt. 17:20)

How can we believe that? First, let us consider what kind of mountain it was which the disciples had failed to remove, hard as they had tried. That mountain, we find, was a severe case of epilepsy, which the Christ readily 'removed' through His great love, triggered by His dauntless faith — a profound trust in God. But the startling thing is that He assures us that if we have a mustard seed kind of faith we can go and do likewise!

Now in the moving of physical mountains people need faith, but they usually harness that faith to earth-moving machinery. As someone wrote a generation ago concerning the construction of the Panama Canal: "A man went down to Panama, where many a man had died, to slit the sliding mountains, and lift the eternal tide. A man stood up in Panama, and the mountains stood aside."

But the most ominous mountains we face seem to be our pride and prejudices, our resentments and worries, our fears and fantasies. And the Christ showed His genius when He indicated that it takes faith like a grain of mustard seed to remove these obstacles. For the mustard seed has a whole world of potentialities hidden within it. Next note what Jesus said concerning His kingdom in relation to all this: "The kingdom of heaven is like a grain of mustard seed which a man took and sowed in his field. It is the smallest of all (then known) seeds, but when it has grown it is the greatest of shrubs and becomes a tree, so that the birds of the air come and make nests in its branches." (Matt. 13:31-32) But notice that the farmer has sense enough to sow or plant the seed in his field. For, with all its tremendous potential, the seed remains dormant until it is planted, and thus exposed to the warmth of the sun's rays, plus the moisture and nurturing elements in the soil.

Isn't this saying to us that we must not only have this quality of faith, but that we must also put it to work and let it grow, before it demonstrates its marvels? But there is a far different concept of faith, totally unlike the mustard seed in that it is quite incapable of such growth and fruitage.

This brittle kind of faith, so called, is spelled out in the book of Jude, verse 3, where we are admonished "to contend for the faith which was once for all delivered to the saints." This has no reference to something vital and ready for growth. Rather, this refers to a body of doctrine, external to us, and which is static, not intended for growth, or even change. Unfortunately, many theologians and religious leaders have latched on to this idea and are busy contending for such a brittle body of doctrine. This constitutes a set of dogmas, with such fear-motivated teachings as the 'infallibility of the Bible', etc. at the center. They see such doctrines as fundamental to what they think of as the one and only true religion. Such creeds are buttressed by sacrament and ritual as the only possible way to 'salvation'. And, true to the admonition to 'contend' for this 'faith once for all delivered to the saints', the contention becomes a bit strident and fearful at times.

But what did Christ say when He was asked what was most important or fundamental? Remember that He gave us this healing word: "You shall love the Lord your God with all your heart, and with all your soul, and with all your mind. This is the great and first commandment. And a second is like it, you shall love your neighbor as yourself." Then He added: "On these two commandments depend all the law and the prophets." (Matt. 22:37-40)

So here we have two sharply contrasting concepts of what religious or spiritual life is all about. One is set (like concrete) in a rigid list of so-called fundamental doctrines, implemented through sacraments and ritual. The other is centered in true love to God and to all humanity, implemented by a vital faith — a seed-like faith — which is really a deep spirit of trust in the basic goodness of life. This is a miracle-working faith which is today being planted in the fertile soil of human need. It is being put to work to remove all obstructing 'mountains', and thus bring in the glad New Age of sharing, justice and peace.

The Christ today is calling on us to do our part, to act in this kind of living faith. He reminds us: "I require the creation of a certain trust, an expectancy and hope." (Message No. 58) And in Message No. 52 He urges us: "Keep open your heart to the Higher Stream and make yourself a channel for Me. I need many such." And in Message No. 38 He assures us: "My Masters are among you in a new way...sowing the seeds of Love and Trust among the nations."

Thus the choice before us: to contend for an external and crystallized body of doctrines, which constitute in reality a denial of trust; or to launch out with a genuine trust in the cause of Christ, putting our mustard seed faith to work in the soil of aching human need — there to let it bear abundant fruitage of love, justice and peace for all. Thus let us eagerly do our part in implementing the great love and energy of the Hierarchy. In this way we can have a vital part in the real 'salvation' or redemption of all our sisters and brothers everywhere, and the entire planetary life as well.

October 1984

24. Written in Heaven

"Lord," said the disciples in jubilation, "even the demons are subject to us in your name!" What was the cause of their high spirits, their unbounded elation? According to Luke, the third gospel writer, these men had just returned from a highly successful teaching and healing mission. They had been sent out for this work by the Christ. It was in His name and spirit that they had presented themselves to the villagers to whom they went. And to their great surprise they had not only seen the lame get up and walk, and the sick become well, but they also had seen the obsessed become liberated from their oppression, to embrace each other with joy. What success, what victory, what rejoicing! I would have been jubilant too.

Remember, these disciples had not been recruited from the ranks of the priests and rabbis, the religious leaders of the day — the ones who were supposed to have a monopoly on such healing power. No, they came from the ranks of the common people, the laity as we might put it today. They were accustomed to earn their living "by the sweat of their brow" as the writer of Genesis describes it — for instance, through catching and selling fish. So what had happened on this mission was indeed a new and exciting experience for them.

But crashing into their excited jubilation comes this surprising and sobering word from their teacher: "Do not rejoice in this, that the spirits are subject to you, but rejoice that your names are written in heaven." (Luke 10:20) Can't you just hear them, bewildered, saying to one another: "What in the world is He talking about anyway? After all, this is the work He sent us out to do, isn't it?"

What He was talking about constituted not so much a rebuke as a correction or warning. Note how often we are reminded that we are to serve joyously and freely, without being attached or wedded to the desired 'fruits' of our action. So let us take a deep look, let us ponder on that surprising word uttered by Jesus: "Do not rejoice in this, that the spirits are subject to you, but rejoice that your names are written in heaven." Can we not see at least one of the reasons for this admonition? For in this realm of duality in which we live and serve, we meet with both seeming success and seeming failure. And there is a tendency, is there not, to get unduly elated and somewhat 'puffed up' if we meet with such outstanding success as those disciples had on that occasion. But then, our sense of self-worth tends to become identified with and dependent upon our successes. So what happens at the other end of the scale, where we meet with what seems like such abject failure? We can plummet from the heights of elation to the depths of depression 'in nothing flat' as some put it.

On the other hand, if we develop the assurance that we are not only members of the fourth or human kingdom, but in our real nature are members of the fifth kingdom, the Kingdom of Souls (which Jesus called alternately the Kingdom of God or of Heaven) then we have a basic security which no one can take from us, 'come hell or high water' to use a colorful phrase. This is the kind of anchorage the Christ wanted those disciples to have. And when we are responsive to Him, He guides us in the same direction.

In Message No. 127 He gives us this assurance: "My Task is to enlighten all men; to change ignorance into true knowledge and faith; to teach men that behind all that they see stands the One Reality." When we are fully anchored in the One Reality we may not feel so high when everything 'turns up roses'; but neither will we feel so depressed when our dreams turn to ashes. It has been said that we must learn to "treat those two impostors, success and failure, just alike." We can only do that, it seems to me, when we know that, as Jesus put it, our names are written in heaven. That is, when we come to know that we are not creatures of a day, but that we are indeed eternal beings, sparks of the one flame, citizens of that deathless Kingdom of God. Then we need not be depressed if the great Day of Declaration seems unduly delayed; nor discouraged if we fail to get others to see the shining truth which seems so clear to us.

Let us ponder on His closing word from Message No. 101: "May the Divine Light and Love and Power of the One Most Holy God be now manifest within your hearts and minds. May this manifestation take you with Me back to your Source."

November 1984

25. He Who Has Ears to Hear

On one occasion Jesus is reported to have said to His hearers: "You search the scriptures, because you think that in them you have eternal life; and it is they that bear witness to me." (John 5:39) Thus is the Christ ever directing us beyond the printed word to the living word, or source of light and love-wisdom. And just as the scriptures bear witness to the Christ, so do they bear witness to the important truth of rebirth or reincarnation.

It appears that Jesus was both teaching and emphasizing this truth when He said concerning John the Baptist: "All the prophets and the law prophesied until John; and if you are willing to accept it, he is Elijah who is to come." Then to add emphasis and help us to really zero in on His meaning, He added: "He who has ears to hear, let him hear." (Matt. 11:13-15)

This emphatic declaration as to John the Baptist being a reincarnation of Elijah is re-stated in different form in the 17th chapter of the gospel according to Matthew. Jesus had taken Peter, James and John, the most advanced of His disciples, up on a high mountain, meaning a high level of consciousness. There He was transfigured before them in what seems to be a brief and symbolical portrayal of the third initiation. On the way back down the mountain (or coming back to a more usual level of consciousness) these disciples asked him: "Why do the scribes say that first Elijah must come? He replied, 'Elijah does come, and is to restore all things; but I tell you that Elijah has already come, and they did not know him, but did to him whatever they pleased. So also the Son of Man will suffer at their hands.' Then the disciples understood that He was speaking to them of John the Baptist." (Matt. 17:10-13)

These seem to be the most pointed Bible references where we find the Christ (through Jesus) strongly affirming and emphasizing this teaching of rebirth. But there are additional scriptural passages which seem to refer directly or indirectly to this matter. For instance, turning to Job 19:26-7 (King James version) we find this interesting statement attributed to Job: "After my skin worms destroy this body, yet in my flesh shall I see God, whom I shall see for myself, and mine eyes shall behold, and not another." Now it is true that other translations differ and seem to convey other meanings. However, the whole book of Job — according to the most perceptive Bible scholars — is an epic drama portraying the severe tests encountered, leading up to initiation, and the great changes in consciousness brought about through this whole process of initiation. This would indicate that the author of this drama of Job had some real understanding of the Ageless Wisdom, and it seems fair to assume that he might well have made essentially such a statement as that attributed above to Job.

Again, in the so-called wisdom teachings of the Old Testament, in Proverbs 8:22 and following verses, we find this inspiring message: "The Lord created me at the beginning of his work... Before the mountains had been shaped, before the hills, I was brought forth; ...when he established the fountains of the deep, when he assigned to the sea its limit...then I was beside him...rejoicing before him always, rejoicing in his inhabited world, and delighting in the sons of men." More often than not this is ascribed to the abstract principle of wisdom. However, it was an individual doing this writing, making these observations. So he might very well have been referring back to a very early incarnation. Let us recall that the Ageless Wisdom tells us that, in some cases at least, our first experience as human beings goes back to the moon chain, before our earth life. At any rate we need to realize that in our own series of lives, wisdom is increasingly beckoning to us, and has been seeking to alert us to truth for many incarnations.

Turning again to the New Testament, Rev. 3:12, we find: "Him that overcometh will I make a pillar in the temple of my

God, and he shall no more go out." Does this not refer to that future time when we will have worked through all our problems and will not need to go out into more incarnations in order to further our progress?

I must confess that there was a time earlier in this present life when I blandly assumed that at least some persons might attain to this high pinnacle in one short life. But I had serious doubts about my own ability to make it. In those days I had no conscious understanding of reincarnation. So when I read Jesus' startling statement in Matt. 5:48: "You, therefore, must be perfect, as your heavenly father is perfect," I was deeply troubled by what seemed to be an unreasonable demand; something impossible of attainment. Now I realize that He was referring indirectly to rebirth, so that we have whatever number of lives we need to achieve that high standard of perfection.

Looking to the Bible some people, it seems, are distressed to find that Jesus did not give us, through the gospels, more direct instruction on this important subject of rebirth. But from remarks I often hear, it seems that many people believe that He did give us more on the subject, and that it was deleted from the Bible at that famous, or infamous, church council meeting at Constantinople in 553 A.D.

Joseph Head and S. L. Cranston, in their well-researched book, *Reincarnation, the Phoenix Fire Mystery*, throw a quite different light on what happened there. Backed up by thorough historical research, they affirm that what that council did was not to change the Bible in any way, but rather to decree that the teaching of pre-existence was anathema. This curse or anathema was pronounced against the teachings of the earlier church father, Origen, who had been about the foremost teacher of reincarnation in the early church. This had the effect of making it against church doctrine to teach pre-existence or reincarnation in the church from this time on. (For further information on this see the section on pp. 156-160 in *The Phoenix Fire Mystery*.)

But this curse or anathema has not stopped entirely the teachings of this important subject in Christianity. From time to time courageous leaders have come forth to express their thoughts on this matter. Among the more recent of these are the late Albert Schweitzer of Europe and Africa, and the late Leslie Weatherhead of England. "Truth, crushed to earth, will rise again," as has so well been said. Is this why Head and Cranston call reincarnation the 'Phoenix Fire Mystery'?

Turning again to the question of why Jesus did not give more attention in His teaching to this matter of rebirth, the most obvious reason is that there did not appear to be the need for such emphasis, because it was so widely accepted among the people of that time and place. Let me quote some evidence in support of this thesis.

In the 16th chapter of Matthew we read where on a certain occasion Jesus asked His disciples what people thought of His identity. They replied that some thought him to be Elijah, some Jeremiah, or one of the other ancient prophets. This clearly indicates a widespread belief among the populace in the doctrine of reincarnation. Likewise in John 1:21 we find that the religious leaders of the time inquired of John the Baptist whether he was Elijah or 'the prophet' (referred to in Deut. 18:15). Does this not indicate that the religious leaders of the time also believed in rebirth?

Further, in the ninth chapter of John we find Jesus and His disciples encountering a man "blind from his birth." Whereupon the disciples inquired of Jesus: "Rabbi, who sinned, this man or his parents, that he was born blind?" Obviously they would not have asked such a question unless they believed that the man born blind had lived before, and now might be meeting the karma or result of sin in a previous life or lives.

So, in these three examples we find evidence that both the general populace, the religious leaders of the time, and also Jesus' disciples had some belief in rebirth. Small wonder then, that Christ at that time chose to give His main emphasis to more pressing matters. The greatest of these major teachings was, as we can see, real love of the Soul level; God's unswerving love to us, and the importance of our loving God with all our heart, Soul, mind, and strength; and loving our neighbors as ourselves. Another urgent emphasis of His was the importance of the individual (or Soul). He took great pains to raise the importance of those previously neglected persons — women and children.

It is interesting to note that, in the Christ's Messages, He calls attention to His own earlier incarnations by reminding us that He has been with us many times before, and He adds: "Try to accept that your Brother of Old is among you." In the wisdom teachings that the Master DK has given us through Alice A. Bailey, we are assured that this time around, during the Aquarian Age, the Christ will definitely teach reincarnation. In the meantime, as we look to the Bible with reference to this matter, let us be grateful for the few clear affirmations on rebirth we find there, plus all the other references which clearly indicate how well those people at that time accepted these important truths. (Do we realize that many of us may well have been numbered among them in an earlier incarnation of our Soul?)

So we may well inquire: do we in our Western world at this time have some catching up to do? Surely it is so in this and many other important and basic truths! So if we have ears to hear, let us hear the Christ in His great love and wisdom calling us now into deeper partnership with Him. Not only that we may better understand these laws of rebirth and cause and effect, but that we may be fully involved in His cause — the cause of love and justice, sharing and brotherhood. We sense the urgency as we realize that this cause involves both the survival of life on this planet earth, and also the lifting of that life into ever more beautiful and meaningful expression; as we go on from our present to higher levels of consciousness; and as we pass on from our present incarnation to the more glorious lives ahead of each of us; and humanity as a whole.

January 1985

26. No Weeds Shall Grow

"My Teaching goes forth. Simple it is, but remember, My friends, it embodies the Plan of God. Where the Plan takes root no weeds shall grow." Such is the surprising assurance the Christ gives us in His Message No. 111.

To get the full impact of the surprise element in this tremendous promise, let us see it in contrast with His parable of weeds and wheat — which He gave us long ago through Jesus in Palestine. In that dramatic word picture He tells us of the man who sowed good seed in his field. But while the man slept his enemy came and sowed weeds among the wheat. (Note the beautiful symbolism here; for it is while we are asleep spiritually that the 'weeds' get their start.) His servants, fearing that the weeds would crowd out the wheat, asked their master's permission to pull out the weeds. But he replied: "No, lest in gathering the weeds you root up the wheat along with them. Let both grow together until the harvest; and at harvest time I will tell the reapers: Gather the weeds first and bind them in bundles to be burned, but gather the wheat into my barn." (Matt. 13:24-30)

So now let us realize that we are in the harvest time of the Piscean Age — the last days of that 2,100 year period. If we have eyes to see we will realize that the harvest of all the 'wheat' grown during that old age is happening all around us. And we can also see the other side of this parable-prophecy being fulfilled before our eyes. For the process of the burning up of the weeds which have grown so furiously has indeed begun. We might add that the fire of burning is getting hotter all the time!

How reassuring it is to be told on such high authority that, in this New Age, where God's Plan takes root "no weeds shall grow." The meaning of this may be difficult for us to fathom at first. We have grown so accustomed to the weeds, it is hard to visualize a weed-free world field! The key phrase in all this is: "Where the Plan takes root." This indicates that it will be an ongoing process, not an overnight happening.

How do you and I help to speed up this process? One of the most urgent things we have to do, it seems to me, is to eradicate the weeds from our own garden spot, or life field. One family or grouping of such harmful weeds is that of fear, along with its more subtle and chronic forms: worry and anxiety. Which of us has not been aware of such noxious growths in our garden? Personally, when I look at my own glamors, I realize that at times I have enhanced their growth — watering them with my attention, and nurturing them with my nervous thoughts — focused on trivial things of the lower self (or not-self as some teachers call it).

The teachers of wisdom tell us, if we will listen, that not by fighting our fears do we get rid of them, but by shifting our attention to the light, love, and power of the Great Ones, and of our own true nature. One of the things I find helpful in this is to read over and over again the Messages from Maitreya. As I turn to these Messages for inspirational help, I find the Christ saying to me: "My help is yours to command. You have only to ask." (Message No. 49) Don't you like that strong word 'command'? His great help is ours to command! We have only to ask. Encouraged, I find myself asking with more confidence. As a result I find His grace progressively pouring in and burning up my weeds ---- really eradicating them.

Many times the weeds take other forms, such as hostility, with its milder but persistent offspring of resentment and irritation. We could go on listing many other forms of noxious weeds which have shown such rank growth during the Piscean Age. Among these are authoritarianism, separatism, and pride, as well as pride's opposite — feelings of inferiority and lack of self-esteem, to name some of the more persistent ones.

Let us remember that the treatment for these is like that for fear and anxiety: not to water them with our tears and guilt, nor feed them with our fixed attention. But rather we are to let them be burned away by the fire of spirit. We do this as we open ourselves and our world to that light, love and power which is increasingly available, through increased use of the Great Invocation (see p. 201), and through the ongoing process of the externalization of the Christ and the Masters.

Let us then bask in this light. Let us serve in this love, in realization of our true stature as sons and daughters of the Most High. Let us also invoke this divine power. These divine energies will bring us into true focus, to fulfill our real purpose in life. In this way we will be doing our part to help humanity fulfill its true destiny also.

March 1985

27. A Future Bathed in Light

In His recent Messages to us, the World Teacher constantly emphasizes the centrality of love, justice and sharing in the divine Plan which He comes to implement. In my re-reading of most of these inspiring Messages, I have discovered how frequently He also emphasizes the great principle of light, or enlightenment for us all.

In Message No. 112, for instance, from which the title of this article is taken, He assures us: "My Promise is this: for all men dawns a future bathed in the Light of God's Truth. Harken to that Truth, My friends, and prove this to be so."

This theme, reiterated for us in so many of His communications, is fully in line with this same emphasis on light which He gave us long ago through Jesus. One of several gospel passages where this is clearly indicated is found in John 8:12, where we read: "I am the light of the world; he who follows me will not walk in darkness, but will have the light of life." In John 14:6 He words this assurance a bit differently when He declares: "I am the way, and the truth, and the life." In that same verse He adds a statement too often misunderstood as He says: "No man comes unto the Father but by me."

Sadly enough, this has been interpreted by many as excluding from the Father, or from heaven, all who have not been converted to the Christian Church through accepting Christian baptism and Christian doctrine. If we have any real understanding of the Christ and His universal outreach, we see that this is not what it means at all. Interestingly enough these words were not even spoken to Christians, for at that point the Christian Church had not yet been organized. That word was spoken to His immediate disciples who were, of course, members of the Jewish faith.

Truly that message He gave is indeed universal in scope, intended for all who climb life's mountain by way of any of the many routes to the top. For whether we are Jew or Gentile, Christian or Moslem, or a member of no religious body at all, the requirement is the same: through self-discipline, meditation, and selfless service we have to rise from our personal levels of endeavor up through Him in order to reach the Father. Another way of saying it is that we have to rise through the buddhic or love-wisdom level of knowing before we can arrive at the monadic level, which is the Father within — the true divine Self.

It was because the meaning of this phrase, "No man cometh unto the Father but by me," was so sadly misinterpreted that, shortly after the death of Mohandas K. Gandhi, an orthodox Christian missionary in India was heard to say: "Isn't it too bad that poor Mr. Gandhi is in hell right now." Shocking as that mistaken statement was, we must recognize it as being right in line with the all-too-usual misunderstanding of that saving word of the Christ, and of His whole nature and message.

It is, of course, well known that Gandhi was a devout Hindu, and one with a wide understanding and tolerance of other forms of religion. His understanding was of such a nature that he well understood he had no need to yield to the persuasions of his Christian friends to be baptized a Christian. So he consistently refused to do so. Yet he had such a high regard for and devotion to the Christ that he had the cross of Christ displayed on the wall of his nearly barren spinning room, along with the words 'He is our peace'. Which one of us would dare claim, or even think, that we have more of that love-wisdom or Christ consciousness in our heart and mind than Gandhi had in his outstanding life and service?

Perhaps it is significant that this truth about coming to the Father through the Christ is reiterated, with slightly different wording, in Message No. 69. There we read: "I guard the Gates through which all pass to Him [God — HRC]." And there too is the context for that affirmation: "When you see Me, My brothers and friends, you will join with Me in a great manifestation of God's Love and create in the world a new Truth, a new Light, a new and shining City of Love. My Task is to lead you therein and perform for you the requirements of God. I guard the Gates through which all pass to Him." Hopefully the people who read these recent communications will not as likely be fooled into putting a narrow and restrictive interpretation upon them.

As for Maitreya's promise concerning a future bathed in light, scores of quotations could be given to amplify that theme, providing other insights and assurances. The other side of this coin, of course, is that you and I will do our part in preparing His way, and in helping to implement the Plan: "My heart aches for those who needlessly suffer now, when so little change could remedy their lot... My Plans involve you all. All who are ready to go with Me into the New Time are called. Help Me, My friends, to reconstruct your world, and send it on its Mission of Light.

"The time is short when you will see Me. Make best use of this little time to tell your brothers of My Presence. There is naught that you could do more valuable than this. Hope rises, My friends. Hope is in your midst. A new Light dawns in the world, and mankind shall know Joy. May the Divine Light and Love and Power of the One Most Holy God be now manifest within your hearts and minds. May this manifestation lead you to see the future in terms of Joy." (Message No. 112)

April 1985

28. A Present Day Parable on Karma and Forgiveness

A certain man had a teenage son who had started on the path of drug abuse. When the father asked him about this, the lad blew up in a rage. He jumped in his shiny new sports car which his family had given him for his birthday, gunned it down the driveway, and sped away, vowing that he never would darken that doorway again.

In the big city he lived a life of luxury and idleness, eventually selling his expensive car for money to support his habit. With things going from bad to worse, he eventually landed on skid row, along with many other unfortunates. Finally, sick and discouraged, he found shelter in a skid row mission, where he was given food, shelter and counseling.

Using strong persuasion, the counselor prevailed on the young man to put in a collect call to home. Before he had time to confess his need and his shame, his father interrupted the phone call to say with enthusiasm: "I will wire you right now the money for a plane ticket home, and I will be waiting for you at the airport. I love you, son, and have prayed for you every day."

The father provided the best possible program of rehabilitation for his son. Improvement came slowly. In time some of the damage to his brain, his liver and kidneys was reversed, but not all of it. With limited capacity he found himself unable to prepare for a position in the legal profession, which had been his dream. But after many setbacks and much difficulty, he was at last able to get into the work of helping other drug addicts.

Suppose, however, that his father had been unforgiving, and had shouted into the phone: "Never show your face here again. You no longer are my son." How long do you suppose it would have taken the son to complete his downward spiral to complete physical destruction? This parable is presented in an effort to show the relationship between forgiveness and the law of cause and effect. When we are in touch with our true Selves, both principles are at work harmoniously in our lives, with the assurance of forgiveness lifting us to a higher level of experience where karma can be paid off rapidly and with much greater ease.

But too many adherents of Christian churches are taught a sadly distorted view of forgiveness. Many believe that God's forgiveness completely wipes out the consequences of wrong doing, providing an easy way out, abrogating the law of cause and effect, so the individual is thought to go 'scot free'. This in spite of the fact that the New Testament plainly teaches: "Be not deceived, God is not mocked. For whatsoever a man soweth, that shall he also reap." (Gal. 6:7)

On the other hand, some persons today who have accepted the idea of karma seem to believe there is no place for forgiveness in life's scheme of things. Both these opposite conclusions are indeed sad distortions (or denials) of the truth.

When I visualize Jesus upon the cross, I hear Him praying for those who have placed Him there and are now railing at Him. He is saying, "Father forgive them, for they know not what they do." I know that word is extended to me also — and it lifts me to a new level of hope, of assurance and of encouragement, where I can cope with everything. Of course I know that the law of cause and effect still holds true — that I am still responsible for my thoughts, words, and actions. But now I know that the universe is not against me, but with me. So with a song in my heart I can work through all my debts on a new level, with divine help all the way. What a difference!

The difference is this: when a person has not experienced the loving grace or forgiveness of God he feels he is 'behind the eight ball'. How can he escape damnation? But when he comes to the place where he experiences God's forgiveness, he is able to forgive his brothers and forgive himself. Now he has self-esteem and knows that however difficult the path, all experiences now work together for good in his life.

How does this fit with the law of cause and effect? It fits perfectly, for now a new cause has entered the equation, dramatically altering the effect. Why do so many people appear to be unready to experience this boon of forgiving love? Perhaps it is because they are so deeply embedded in their fears and guilts. So, they continue to wallow in a very painful morass of karma. Fortunately, however, the force of evolution will eventually bring them through to a new level of awareness, where they can experience the healing power of forgiveness. Then the equation of cause and effect will be dramatically changed for the better and they can pay off their debts with the fortification of divine love. Then the progress to freedom will be much more rapid.

On the little family farm in Michigan where I grew up, there was a small swampy area in the pasture lot. The cattle seemed instinctively to avoid that area. One day when I started out across it I found that with each step I would sink into the mire halfway to my knees. The going was very slow and, when I finally emerged, I was exhausted. Putting my feet once more on solid ground felt indeed like an emancipation. To me, that slow and painful walk through the swamp is analogous to the slow and painful process of trying to cope with karma on a level where we feel guilty and unforgiven; whereas, walking with ease on solid ground is like dealing successfully with our karma when we experience the gracious forgiving love of God, which allows us to forgive ourselves.

As I study the many Messages of the Christ I find many assurances of love, light, and divine help for us all. And I find nothing to indicate that the Christ is here to administer wrathful judgment. Let me quote a few of His assuring words given in Messages No. 67 and 136: "Many there are who fear My advent. The guilt of ages rests upon their shoulders and they trust not. My friends, through Me shall be created the era of trust, the removal of guilt, the citadel of love... When you see Me, fear not — I come not to scold but to teach. There are those among you who await Me as a judge and fear My coming. Naught that I say shall disappoint you; naught that I do shall cause you fear."

What beautiful assurance He gives us. So let us realize that karma and forgiveness fit together like hand and glove, and that the experience of forgiveness lifts us to a new dimension of life — where we are in direct partnership with Him — and His gracious love aids us beyond measure in our climb up the steep side of life's mountain.

May 1985

29. Hell or Heaven — We Make Our Own

It is reported that Mark Twain, on being asked what he thought of heaven and hell, replied, "I'm not going to tell you ---- for I have friends in both places." I could go him one better, for I have had experiences in both places; or rather, experiences in both such levels of consciousness.

For surely it is high time to graduate from the outgrown concept of heaven as an area 12,000 furlongs square, set apart somewhere in space. Likewise we need to shake ourselves free of the superstition of hell as an inferno, partitioned off in subterranean space where we are in danger of being fried for all eternity, having been sentenced thereto by an external deity. To this hell we are supposedly sent as penalty for some such offense as failure to be baptized in a Christian ceremony, or failure to accept the brittle theology set forth by some Christian churches.

Let us take a look at these two familiar concepts: first, the notion of hell, and then of heaven. One Greek word which is translated as 'hell' in our English Bibles is 'gehenna', said to be derived from 'ge-hinnom'. Gehenna, we are told, was a smoldering garbage heap outside Jerusalem, the holy city. It was there that cast-off decaying matter continued to smoulder and burn ("where the worm dieth not, and the fire is not quenched." Mark 9:46)

Perhaps this is a fitting symbol for the smoldering fires of resentment, hostility and hatred which we coax into flame within us when we choose to live outside the holy city of divine love and grace. Then later, when we come to face our responsibility for creating this smoldering mess of hostility or hatred, the fires become much more intense and painful, taking the form of acute burning remorse.

The other term often used to describe the hellish experiences we create for ourselves is the word 'darkness'. Jesus is said to have described this condition as 'outer darkness', where "there shall be weeping and gnashing of teeth." (Matt. 8:12) I believe it is one of the Masters, probably DK, who points out that men turn their backs to the light and walk in their own shadows, then complain that it is dark.

How true this is. The shadows can be pretty deep. The darkness we create for ourselves is only the absence of the light on which we have turned our backs. So the darkness is but an illusion. Yet I know by experience that the fears, anxieties and worries we conjure up can seem very real and threatening. But if we make the decision, we can turn around, face the light, and walk in its radiance. It really is a matter of choice.

Easter, which we experience as a particular day in April, is a prime symbol of this profound change. And we need to realize that without waiting for the calendar to present us with another day called Easter, we can right now walk out of our little self-made tombs of darkness. All that is needed is to invite the angels of our better nature to roll away the heavy stone of our distrust we have so carefully placed there, then summon the courage to walk out into the light of love, joy and divine purpose, which is heaven indeed.

As we do this, one big surprise may await us. For while the hell we have fashioned in our consciousness is our own private hell, the heaven we dare to claim — if it is real — is not separate or private at all. For it has no walls of separation, no boundaries or outer limits. It is the experience we enter when we are ready to love all beings, to share all resources and to walk the path of unselfish service. It is the blessed experience of oneness with all.

As Sai Baba has said: "Through Love you can visualize Truth. Love God and you see God in every creature." (*Sai Baba Avatar,* p. 184) And in Christ's Message, while not using the words heaven and hell, He clearly sets forth the sharp contrast between these opposite levels of experience as He asks us:

"Where are you going, My friends? Are you with Me or forever against Me and your brother; for My Task is to show you that the way for man is the sure Path of Love. Through Justice and Sharing, that Love, My brothers, will become mani- fest. Take heed, then, of My words.

"Look within and find the readiness to share. Remove from your shoulders the weight of guilt and suffering. Remove forever the curse of separation, of loneliness and fear. Take heed, My friends, and do this — do this now. Know that My Love will support you. My Law will guide you. My Teaching will show you the future for all men, a future bathed in the light of Living Truth. Take Me to your hearts, My friends, and know Me as a brother. Manifest that which I am and recreate the world. Lift yourselves by My Love into the lap of God." (Message No. 117)

Let us together walk with joy in this heavenly way, with the Christ and all our brothers and sisters.

June 1985

30. "That All Men May Quench Their Thirst"

The Christ is bidding us: "Take your place at My side, and work as never before. Help Me, My friends, to create a pool of Love so deep that all men may quench their thirst."

For what do men thirst? Obviously for many things. First of all, the thirst for money — for material wealth — seems like an epidemic. Maitreya has pointed out how the rich parade their wealth before the poor and starving. But it becomes evident that no matter how successful this quest may be, it leads at day's end to a dry well — a pitiful emptiness.

Finding that search for acquisition of wealth not fulfilling, many seek to quench their thirst at some pinnacle of honor: winning the gold cup, the blue ribbon, the doctorate in multiple fields, the presidency of state or industrial conglomerate, or what have you. These are a few of the high altitudes at which men think to quench that basic thirst to which all members of the human race are subject.

A close relative (perhaps a twin) of the chase for honor is the urge for power over other people's lives. Such power, on the part of the frustrated, is often sought at the point of a gun. Robbing someone, and more especially shooting unarmed victims, is said to give a temporary feeling of great power. God gives the precious gift of life in order that we as Souls may grow and develop through experience here in the physical body. The media record daily how very often some recipients of that gift of life seek power by brutally terminating the lives of other persons. In the same thrust for power we see nations seeking domination over other nations by building bigger and ever more threatening stockpiles of destructive weapons — to hold as a threat in the Russian roulette game of international power politics.

But not all seekers of power travel such obviously destructive bypaths on the journey of life. The power of a forceful and selfish will is often used to dominate a family, control a religious organization, or sway a nation. For a time such power, used over others, seems in a measure to quench the deep thirst of some individuals for fulfillment. But history's epitaph of the Alexanders, the Caesars, the Napoleons, the Hitlers and the Mussolinis tells a sad and far different story. Yes, the drive for separative power over other lives ends finally in futility and ashes.

We could look at some of the other means by which people seek to satisfy that insistent thirst for fulfillment of life's meaning and purpose. Among these cul-de-sacs are such avenues as the search for unfailing comfort; the search for pleasure through travel; the quest for substitute and artificial body parts, related to the demand for long years of dwelling in the 'prison house of the physical body', as it is designated in the Ageless Wisdom. (George Burns avers that when you reach the age of 100 years you are pretty safe, for, statistically, very few people die after that age!) But note that all these separative 'watering places' prove finally to be dry wells of bitter disappointment.

It is in reference to such weary quests that the writer of Ecclesiastes (the most pessimistic book in the Bible) refers: "Vanity of vanities, says the Preacher, all is vanity. What does a man gain by all the toil at which he toils under the sun? A generation goes and a generation comes... The sun rises and the sun goes down, and hastens to the place where it rises. The wind blows to the south, and goes round to the north; round and round goes the wind, and on its circuits the wind returns... All things are full of weariness; a man cannot utter it; the eye is not satisfied with seeing, nor the ear with hearing. What has been is what will be, and what has been done is what will be done; and there is nothing new under the sun... I have seen everything that is done under the sun; and behold, all is vanity and a striving after wind."

So where are we to turn for the quenching of our thirst — the thirst for meaning, for fulfillment, which we share with all our sisters and brothers? What a source of encouragement it is to find in our day more and more people are turning to Maitreya, the Christ, for the answer to life's riddle.

Long ago, as we read in the fourth chapter of the gospel according to John, He gave out a saving word concerning 'the water of life' which He gives to those who seek him and His way. According to that account Jesus was resting beside Jacob's well near the Samaritan city of Sychar, when a Samaritan woman came to draw water. In that culture it was unheard of for a man to speak to a strange woman. Also we read that "the Jews had no dealings with the Samaritans," so He was violating two taboos when He spoke to this woman. In the course of the conversation Jesus explained to her: "Everyone who drinks of this water (from the well) will thirst again, but whoever drinks of the water that I shall give him will never thirst; the water that I shall give him will become in him a spring of water welling up to eternal life."

Incidentally, it appears worthy of note that not only did Jesus converse with this apparently outcast Samaritan, who had been married five times and was then living with a man to whom she was not married, but He also gave her what amounted to an evangelistic mission: to go and bring her townspeople out to hear Him, that they also might find the secret of the water of life which quenches all thirst.

Often I hear people, objecting to the idea of the Christ's presence in a physical body in our world, say something like this: "I don't think we can expect any one person to do it alone." If they would only read just a few of the Messages they would discover how grossly mistaken is the idea that He is here to do the needed work alone, and how repeatedly He calls for our work, our co-operation with Him much as Jesus called for the Samaritan's help.

Let me repeat that on 18 December 1980, the Christ challenged us: "Help Me, My friends, to create a pool of Love so deep that all men may quench their thirst." And He explains: "My Teaching is simple — Justice and Love, Sharing and Peace will bring men to God." This is the way of enduring fulfillment; but as He says over and over again, He is only the architect and we must be the willing builders of the temple of truth.

He is calling to us all to help Him create this unlimited pool of love where all men may quench the thirst we all share for meaning and fulfillment. If we tune into Him, He will — as promised — show us how and where we may do our part in His great work for our day and our world.

July 1985

31. Biblical Teachings and the Great Initiations

In the June 1985 issue of *Share International,* Benjamin Creme's Master has assured us: "It is not long until the world will see the Christ... Take heart from this promise, for the day is not far off when men's anguish will be assuaged... For the tide is turning in favour of the light."

So it behooves us to give prime attention to the basic wisdom teachings which the Christ and the Masters hold to be important. Again Creme's Master informs us that "Among the many procedures of which they [the Masters — HRC] make use, that known as initiation is the most important." (*Share International,* May 1985) Since many of us have a background in Christian teaching from the Bible, I have been encouraged to write on biblical teaching as it relates to the five great initiations leading to Mastership. Please note that this and the following chapters on this subject are not an attempt to set forth a classical or definitive treatise on initiation. That would take volumes. Besides, this would be beyond my present capacity and has already been done by Alice A. Bailey and others. What I am proposing to do is much more modest: to show how the Bible, and especially the gospel accounts, point — often in a veiled manner — to these great initiatory experiences.

Briefly, the stories of the birth of Christ at Bethlehem symbolize the first initiation. The baptism at the river Jordan symbolizes the second great initiation, which is baptism into greater responsibility with higher consciousness. The transfiguration on the mountain top points to the third initiation, when our whole personality or lower nature is to be under the control or direction of the Soul or higher nature. The trial at Jerusalem, culminating in the crucifixion, symbolizes the fourth initiation, often called the Great Renunciation. The resurrection from the tomb beautifully portrays the fifth initiation, completing the long process of transition from the fourth or human kingdom to the fifth, which Jesus called the Kingdom of God or of Heaven, making the initiate a Master of Wisdom, or a 'full grown man in Christ', as the Bible puts it.

Ensuing chapters will deal with the Bible and the later initiations.

Let us now look briefly at the first initiation as seen from the Ageless Wisdom, an initiation often hidden in the Bible. Those who are familiar with the gospel according to John will recall that a certain 'ruler of the Jews', a man named Nicodemus, came to Jesus by night to inquire about His work. In the course of the conversation Jesus is reported to have said to this pharisee: "Truly, truly I say to you, unless one is born anew, he cannot see the Kingdom of God." And a bit later He emphasized: "Truly I say to you, unless one is born of water and the Spirit, he cannot enter the Kingdom of God. That which is born of the flesh is flesh, and that which is born of the Spirit is spirit. Do not marvel that I said to you: you must be born anew." (John 3:3, 5-7) Clearly Jesus was pointing out to Nicodemus that the New Birth, the first initiation, is the first and a most essential step into the fifth kingdom, the Kingdom of God.

Much has been written, by Geoffrey Hodson and others, as to how the birth stories about Jesus, recorded only in Matthew and Luke, are really symbolic of the first initiation, a life-changing experience toward which all of us are moving unless we have indeed been through it in this or a previous life. Be it noted that Matthew and Luke are the only New Testament writers who mention the birth of Jesus at all. And their accounts are widely divergent. Matthew's report is that of the Christmas star, seen in the east; of the wise ones who followed that star; their inquiry of king Herod; their presentation of gold, frankincense and myrrh to the new babe; and of Herod's angry and murderous response. But no trip from Nazareth to Bethlehem is mentioned. Luke, on the other hand, tells of shepherds, "keeping watch over their flocks by night"; of the angelic message "Behold I bring you good news of a great joy which will come to all the people..." and of the heavenly chorus singing "Glory to God in the highest, and on earth peace among men with whom he is pleased." It also tells of the shepherds going into Bethlehem and finding the mother and child, with the 'babe lying in a manger'. All of this after Mary and Joseph had made the long trip from Nazareth to Bethlehem for the census-taking decreed by the Roman emperor.

In Matthew's account the three wise men can symbolize the three adepts who are said to be present at the first initiation, which is usually taken in an out-of-body experience while the physical body is asleep, perhaps half a world away. Later, after the Christ's Day of Declaration, we are informed that He will make preparations to act as Hierophant (initiator) for the first and second initiations right here on the physical plane for those who have, probably through many lives, made sufficient preparation — through building good character, overcoming the habits of lust, gluttony, and other physical indulgences. The Masters, we are told, can tell by reading our aura, exactly when we are ready for initiation, and when our karma permits.

The three gifts presented by the Magi can symbolize the presentation of the three aspects of our lower nature (physical, astral, and mental) to God through initiation. And Herod can symbolize the attempt of our lower nature to destroy the new Christ-consciousness born in our heart center. The lower nature is ever on guard against giving up its age-old reign over our life. So we must be vigilant and identify with our infant Christ-nature, rather than with the old and discredited 'Herod-nature'.

In Luke's account, the shepherds, keeping watch over their flocks 'by night', can symbolize for us those members of humanity who, though not yet fully enlightened, are alert enough, even amidst darkness, to attune themselves to the angel song and catch the healing word of peace and goodwill.

The stable in which Jesus is reported to have been born is said by many to have been a cave, since many stables of that time and country were indeed caves. All the four kingdoms of our ordinary evolution are represented there: the mineral kingdom by the rocks and soil; the plant kingdom by the hay and fodder; the animal kingdom by the animals sheltered there; the human kingdom by Mary and Joseph. Even the fifth kingdom is represented by the newborn Christ, the Bethlehem babe. The account of the babe born in a stable among the animals can symbolize the fact that such an initiation has to take place, not between incarnations, but while we are living the physical life, with the higher vehicles encased in our physical nature.

There is much more symbolism which could be traced in these biblical stories of the birth at Bethlehem (the house of bread), which indicates that what we are really celebrating at the festival of Christmas, if we are alert to the Ageless Wisdom, is this wondrous festival of New Birth, the first initiation. And this insight can alert us also to the importance, not just at Christmas time but at all times, of making due preparation for whichever initiation lies ahead of us. Let us be about 'our Father's business', as Luke indicates Jesus certainly was, through re-dedicating all of our thought and life to Him; presenting our gifts through a life of meditation, sharing, and whole-hearted Soul-level service.

September 1985

(Note: Most of the information in these chapters on initiation is based on the Alice A. Bailey books, and therefore I am indebted to her and to the Master DK for these insights. But, as far as possible, I have tried to put the material into words of my own choosing and vocabulary. —HRC)

32. The Second Initiation in the Bible

Just as in the gospel account the first initiation is symbolized by the birth of the babe at Bethlehem, so is the second initiation indicated by Jesus' baptism at the river Jordan. This, we note, is said to have happened a long time (30 years) after the birth, and points to the fact that a long span of time, usually several incarnations, intervenes between the first and second initiations.

Such a significant event, of course, involves much more than mere baptism by water. The real ceremony, according to the Ageless Wisdom, takes place high on the inner planes, while the physical body is asleep. So the biblical account of Jesus' baptism is but an outer symbol of a far-reaching change of consciousness taking place within, and since water is the most common symbol for the astral or emotional plane, the biblical account of immersion in water is most appropriate.

In the esoteric literature it is well established that the second initiation can be undergone only after a long and difficult struggle with personal desires and emotions, culminating in a large measure of Soul mastery over this 'watery' sphere. In Jesus' case this mastery undoubtedly was symbolically achieved during the first thirty years of His life while He was subjected to the stresses and strains of family life, relating to an ageing father, a saintly mother, and sibling competition with His brothers and sisters. According to tradition, He assumed greater responsibility upon the death of Joseph, becoming male head of the household.

In *The Masters and the Path*, C. W. Leadbeater has an interesting discussion of the three 'fetters' which the first degree initiate must 'cast off' before he is prepared for the Baptism initiation. The first of these fetters is the delusion of the separate self. This has to be replaced by the realization of oneness in the true Self. The second fetter is the glamor of doubt or uncertainty, especially in relation to the truth of reincarnation and karma, or the law of cause and effect. The third fetter is described as superstition, or the belief that the rites and dogma of any one religion are necessary for salvation, or that we have to deal with the so-called 'wrath of an angry God'.

Surely these and any other necessary tests had been met and mastered by Jesus before He presented himself to John the Baptist for baptism at the river Jordan. But from another point of view, since the Ageless Wisdom teaching is that Jesus came into that incarnation as a third-degree initiate, let us realize that Jesus repeated or recapitulated the process of the first three initiations for our benefit ---- the benefit of humanity.

Now let us look more closely at the symbols given to us in the gospel story concerning this event. Since between the first and second initiations we are engaged in a struggle with a tumult of emotions such as resentment, fear, worry and depression, it is indeed appropriate to picture oneself being submerged in the water (the emotions) in preparation for being raised up out of the watery sphere as the victorious climax of that long struggle. Remember, too, that when immersion is undergone it is the officiant who lifts the candidate up out of that watery element in which symbolically all of us have been immersed. Thus we see that, for us, the officiant is our higher nature which lifts us up out of our astral turmoil where we could so easily drown — in fear and depression, for example — for the little personal self has no power of itself to rise to a new element and a higher level of consciousness. Looking at it differently we can see that it is the Christ within us, who has come to birth in our heart center, who lifts us up out of the morass of our troubled emotions.

The dove and the voice are two more important symbols given to us in the gospel account of the event which we are considering. "When Jesus was baptized, he went up immediately from the water, and behold, the heavens opened and he saw the Spirit of God descending like a dove, and alighting on him.

And lo, a voice from heaven, saying, 'This is my beloved son, in whom I am well pleased.'" (Matt. 3:16-17) From ancient times to modern the dove has been the pre-eminent symbol of peace. Thus in the observance of the 40th anniversary of the atomic bombing of Hiroshima, 1,500 doves were suddenly re- leased, rising rapidly into the air, suggesting the urgent thrust of humanity for peace.

And with the triumph of the second initiation, the heaven-sent dove of peace comes down upon us, bringing serenity to the previously troubled waters of the astral body. The heavenly word, "This is my beloved son, in whom I am well pleased," is perhaps even more significant. This means that assurance comes from the inmost Spirit that we really are divine, beloved sons and daughters of God. Let us attune our hearing to that true inner voice. For if we will but listen we will find its divine counsel, given not just at a high moment of initiation, but many other times as well. Remember that the whole time between initiations has been described as an initiatory process.

Some have been puzzled about Jesus' three temptations coming in that wilderness experience immediately after His baptism. There are different ways of looking at this 40-day period. From our point of view let us see the period as the time it took for the inner plane initiatory experience to be stabilized on the physical brain level of active consciousness. That had to happen before Jesus was properly equipped to enter into His active ministry. And it has to happen with us following our second initiation — taking perhaps 40 months or even many years — before the high vibrations and high consciousness of the Baptism experience come to be fully registered in our outer consciousness, so we can properly utilize our transformed and serene astral body in the service we are called upon to give.

After His 40 days of fasting, the first temptation Jesus faced was the suggestion to use the magical divine power attained to turn stones into bread to satisfy His own hunger. And think how often we are likewise tempted to use our increasing insights and powers 'to feather our own nests', so to speak. Let us consider: can we, like Jesus, overcome this temptation by remembering that we really are not this body, and therefore we also are not to live by bread alone but by the word which comes from God, or from the Monad within?

In the second temptation Jesus saw himself on a pinnacle of the temple being tempted to employ astral phenomena — in this case the power of levitation — to come floating down from that pinnacle before the astonished pilgrims making their way to a temple ceremony. This would be an immediate way to gather a large following. But the followers would be a crowd of people fascinated by the magic of astral phenomena instead of a band of men committed to the long hard way of self-sacrifice leading to the cross. This temptation seemed to hold little appeal for Jesus — quite in contrast to the large numbers of people today who are captivated and side-tracked by some glamorous forms of psychic phenomena.

But the third temptation was undoubtedly the most severe for Jesus. It is said this took place on a high mountain, which symbolically means a high level of consciousness. There He was shown all the kingdoms of the world and the glory of them, and was told all this would be His if He would just fall down and worship 'satan'. What a drastic fall that would have been. For it would have meant resorting to political intrigue and military strategy in the attempt to win the world to himself. But at this high level Jesus saw clearly that 'satan' would not be able to deliver on his deceptive promise. For through the clear lens of truth it is clearly seen that there is but one kingdom, not many, toward which humanity is to move, and that is the Kingdom of God. That kingdom is established only through love, which is also the way of the cross.

These three temptations come in many forms and differing garb. But essentially they are the ones we all have to face, perhaps at many times, and especially after the second initiation has been experienced on the high mental planes and we are in the process of seeking to stabilize the newly-attained powers on the outer-plane level of understanding and usage.

Alice Bailey points out that the tempting voice repeatedly said to Jesus: "If you are the Son of God..." And a basic temptation for all of us is that of doubting our sonship, our divinity. Do we dare to deal with the reality that we truly are divine (in our Soul nature)? For once we say "yes" to that challenge, realizing our divinity, then we have to act — to serve — from that high level. We know it is far from easy! But once we are fully committed to that purpose, we have all the help we need from the Hierarchy for achievement.

As Alice Bailey points out (in *From Bethlehem to Calvary,* p. 220): "With Christ, desire was transmuted into Power." So will it be with us when, in His spirit, we walk His way.

October 1985

33. The Third Initiation: Transfiguration

You will remember that, in preparation for the first initiation, the 'sins of the flesh' such as lust, greed and gluttony have to be fairly well conquered so that the higher nature has a high degree of control over the physical body. And that, in preparation for the second initiation, the astral body (meaning the emotional nature) has to be largely mastered, with serenity replacing such emotions as fear, hostility and guilt — emotions which have held sway over that previously stormy, watery astral body for so many lives.

Now, in preparation for the third initiation of the Transfiguration, the mind also has to come under the control and direction of the higher nature so that, by the time we have undergone the third initiation, the Soul will have a large degree of mastery over the whole lower self — physical, astral-emotional and lower mental. As you can imagine, however, this is not achieved without a fierce struggle — between the second and third initiations — to overcome 'illusion', just as there has been a hard struggle with 'glamor' between the first and second initiations.

What is illusion anyway? It has been described as glamor on the mental plane. But more precisely, illusion is distortion of reality on the mental plane (the realm of thinking), just as glamor is distortion of reality on the astral plane — the playground of the emotions. One example of such a distortion or illusion in our thinking is that which leads to pride. Pride is a mental condition in which the lower, separative mind falsely assumes a position or claim of superiority over others — at least over some others.

Now it seems that on the lower level of development we may need some pride to help us overcome our feelings of inferiority; that is, to bolster our weak sense of self-esteem. Indeed, as personalities, we may be further up the ladder than some persons are, and certainly we are not as advanced as some others. But however helpful this illusion of pride might seem to be on the lower rungs of the ladder, by the time we approach the high altitude of Transfiguration, we must come to realize that we are not really personalities at all, but the true Self and part of the One Whole. So where is the ground for any supposition of either superiority or of inferiority? To climb to the place where we have not only overcome the physical demands for the separative self and the glamorous emotions of resentment and fear, but also our mental illusions of pride and grandeur, is a high achievement indeed. The mastery may not be perfectly complete, but it must be nearly so before our Transfiguration takes place.

Let us recall that in Matthew's account of this third initiation (17:1-8) the three disciples present — Peter, James and John — witnessed Jesus completely transfigured before them, His whole being, and even His garments, shining with an intense white light such as they never before had witnessed. Can we come to grips with the realization that at this summit experience we too will be enveloped in this tremendous light and power? For we will for the first time come face to face with God — that is, with Sanat Kumara, the embodiment of the planetary Logos. We need to keep in mind that at the earlier initiations — the divine Birth and the divine Baptism — it is the Lord Christ, Maitreya, who is the Hierophant, the one wielding the Rod of Power and welcoming us to a new level of experience. But by the time of this third initiation we will have made so much progress that it is the incarnate Lord of the World who is the Initiator.

As Alice Bailey reminds us: "An initiation is a blaze of illumination thrown upon the river of existence, and it is in the nature of a whole experience. There is no indefiniteness in it, and the initiate is never quite the same again in his consciousness." (*From Bethlehem to Calvary*, p. 183) The illumination at the third initiation far surpasses any at an earlier time.

For some time now the Ageless Wisdom teachings have been telling us that we are not the physical body, not the emotions, not the lower mind which we call the intellect, nor are we the sum total of these — called the personality, but that these are merely instruments through which we as divine beings choose to work while in physical incarnation. For many of us, however, this teaching has fallen on deaf ears or at best has remained but a theoretical concept. However, when we come to experience this Transfiguration initiation, we will *know* beyond the shadow of a doubt that we are the divine Self, and that the three-fold personality is but a dim reflection of that divinity. Not only will we know this divinity within ourselves, or *as* ourselves, but we will realize also that all our brothers and sisters are indeed sparks of that one divine flame. Alice Bailey quite pointedly remarks in this connection that if man is not divine, then the fatherhood of God is but an empty concept.

The deep reason that, at this initiation, we will know that we are divine is that for the first time we will truly be in touch with our inmost Spirit or Monad. Previous to this, on our long and difficult climb up life's mountain, we have been striving to achieve Soul consciousness, to become a Soul-infused personality. At the third initiation that great achievement will be realized and as that Soul, or Solar Angel, we will begin reaching up toward monadic consciousness, something that may not be fully achieved until we become Masters of Wisdom at the fifth initiation.

In the Jerusalem Bible (which I consider the most accurate of all English translations) we find these words at a high point of the Transfiguration: "This is my Son, the Beloved; he enjoys my favor, listen to him." (Matt. 17:5) When we reach that high level we also will know that 'I and the Father are one', now that there is no barrier between the initiate and the Monad or Father within.

And we too will be conveying the living word of God so clearly that humanity will need to listen.

During that experience Jesus saw the future unfolding before Him with clarity; and not far distant, His coming trial and crucifixion at Jerusalem. So He began preparing His disciples for the crucial test which would also await them at that time. Let us also be prepared to look clearly, when that high experience is ours, into our own future. For we will then have the courage to face whatever testings it has in store for us, knowing that, however hard the path, we will have what it takes to be victorious.

It would be well to recognize, however, that all of these marvellous insights may not be immediately available to us in our outer brain level of consciousness. The reason is that the energies are so tremendous at this third initiation that it may take months or even years for the physical brain to absorb them without brain damage. But though the outer realization may need to come slowly, yet the results of achieving that high level will be beautiful indeed.

From this time on, for example, our service will be free from all selfishness or self-centeredness. This truly will be world service, service of meaning and value for all humanity. We will know when and what to speak, and when to remain silent. Our word will go out with power, and the power of our silent thought will bless the world.

We will realize our freedom from the age-old slavery to the three-fold personality. Thus our experience will include not only all our human brothers and sisters, but all aspects and forms of life. We will be fully aware that we are living a really new life; that we are associated with the Spiritual Hierarchy of our planet earth. With true humility, we will know that together we all become channels through which God can reach and lift humanity step by step out of its bondage. And though this high peak may seem to gleam far, far above us, let us take heart and new courage, and seek the inspiration which will enable us to move steadily onward and upward upon those steps which will lead unfailingly to that great summit.

November 1985

34. The Bible and the Great Renunciation

"Why even think about the fourth initiation?" someone may ask. "It is so far ahead of us, isn't it a waste of time to give any consideration to this great, distant event?" No, indeed. Such consideration, far from being futile, can be quite fruitful. For the little renunciations we make all along the way, if we make them willingly, are stepping stones in preparation for that major step that lies ahead — called by Christians the Crucifixion. So let us look at Jesus' life and teachings, as He prepared His disciples — as well as Himself — for this painful ordeal which might better be thought of as a glorious victory, for such it is.

As we look briefly at some of those preparatory steps, we see that immediately following the transfiguration experience (which symbolizes the third initiation) Jesus began discussing with His disciples His 'decease' which He was 'to accomplish at Jerusalem'. Though even His inner circle of 12 disciples was very slow to comprehend this unwanted teaching — so foreign to their way of thinking — it proved to be of great value to them later, after the event, as they struggled to grasp the significance of what had happened.

About this time also the great difficulties which are said to come in the life of one taking the fourth initiation began to pile up. In the sixth chapter of John we read that many of Jesus' followers began to defect when they heard teachings such as: "It is the spirit that gives life, the flesh has nothing to offer. The words I have spoken to you are spirit and they are life." (verse 63)

We might well inquire whether these words are also a warning to us to consider the meaning and the cost of discipleship — whether our background is labelled Christian, Buddhist or whatever. A further indication that the tide was turning against Jesus as He prepared for the final testings in Jerusalem is found in the fact that now the priesthood of the time began to be hostile to Him. Earlier He had been invited to speak and teach in their synagogues. (See Luke 4:16 ff.) But now, in His later ministry, the scribes and priests became jealous of His popularity and fearful for the future of the tight and profitable little system by which they monopolized their religion. So they accused Him of being possessed and of casting out demons by the power of Beelzebub, prince of demons. Thus the opposition rolled up, and He found the doors of the synagogues closed against His teaching.

But it was the cleansing of the temple early in the last week of His ministry that effectively crystallized the opposition against Him. Why? Because He drove out those who sold sacrificial animals and pigeons at an exorbitant price, and overturned the tables of the money changers who had a high-priced monopoly on the only coins which were accepted for the purchase of the sacrificial animals. So the plot against Jesus thickened, and the Sadducees, the priestly party which controlled the profiteering business in the temple, found themselves in the fortunate position of quickly locating a member of Jesus' inner circle of 12 who was ready to betray his teacher and deliver Him into their hands. (Space does not permit discussion of Judas' possible motives for this act of treachery.)

At the 'Seder' supper or passover meal — called by Christians the Last Supper, the basis for the later ritual of the Eucharist — Jesus sought to prepare His remaining 11 disciples for the tragic events that would occur later that night and the following day — known as Good Friday in the Christian church year. Why is that day so called? Because orthodox theologians make it the key to salvation — according to the substitutionary theory of the atonement. Take note of Jesus' long prayer of consecration uttered during the occasion of that supper and recorded in the 17th chapter of John. It was given for the benefit of the disciples of the time and for all disciples of all time.

After the meal Jesus and the 11 proceeded to the garden of Gethsemane, where He agonized over the well-known prayer which concludes: "Father, not my will but thine be done." From this point on I understand that Jesus was on His own — the three-year overshadowing by the Lord Christ being terminated because it was Jesus who needed to bear the brunt of these acute events which symbolize in the outer life the pivotal inner experience of the fourth initiation.

These events include the Gethsemane struggle; the arrest following the traitorous kiss by Judas; the illegal midnight trial before the high priest and some members of the Sanhedrin — the high court of that time and place; the early morning trial before Pontius Pilate, the Roman governor; the desertion by the remaining 11 disciples — including Simon Peter's triple denial that he knew Jesus; derision and abuse by the Roman soldiers; the scourgings; the derisive crown of thorns; the exhausting trek to Mount Calvary; and the crowning ignominy — crucifixion between two common criminals. If we need a graphic portrayal of the difficulties leading to and the sufferings experienced during the fourth initiation, here we have them spelled out for us in capital letters of love and pain.

And we must include Jesus' compassionate cry from that cross: "Father forgive them for they know not what they do," and His agonized cry, "my God, my God, why hast thou forsaken me?" Some theologians, lacking understanding, have asserted He was merely quoting a psalm, and thus have tried to deny the crucial nature of this cry. He was indeed quoting from the first sentence of what we have labelled Psalm 22. But in so doing, He was uttering the agonized cry of the fourth-degree initiate when, as we are told, all help — objective and subjective — is removed momentarily so that the initiate finds it necessary to come unaided through that crucial stage of utter loneliness. But because He came through it successfully, He was able also to speak those final victorious words from the cross: "It is finished," and "Father, into thy hands I commend my spirit." Thus what was seen by the plotters against Jesus as the crowning ignominy turned out to be His crowning victory.

Two more aspects of the symbolism involved must be emphasized. One, already touched upon, is the prayer, "Father, not my will but thine be done." We, aspirants and disciples who have not advanced that far along the path, may indeed utter this prayer with our lips and our intellects. But it reaches a true level of complete commitment to the divine will at this fourth initiation. Then it is fully effective, and so the secrets and the power of the Father's will (involving the Monad within) become truly operative. From this point on, the initiate effectively channels not only the light and love of God but also the will. Note that these are the three aspects of the higher life we are reaching for in the first three stanzas of the Great Invocation.

The other crucial symbol given us in the gospel account of the Great Renunciation was that at the time of the crucifixion, "the veil of the temple was rent in twain, from top to bottom." What was this veil? In the temple at Jerusalem it was the partition that separated the outer part of the temple from the inner Holy of Holies, as it was called. Esoterically this is a most appropriate symbol. For during the experience of the Great Renunciation the veil of separation between the individual and the inner sanctuary of the Monad — the Father within — is removed. So from that experience onward we will have access to the inner mysteries and powers of life to an amazing degree, such as we have not known before. For when we reach that summit the Waiting Ones know we will utilize these mysteries and powers, not only in completely unselfish ways but in such a manner that great benefit will accrue to humanity. It is hoped that, as we contemplate these tremendous happenings, we will be strengthened and encouraged to take our next steps on the path with love, joy and courage. As the Christ is saying to us through Benjamin Creme (Message No. 130): "My Truth kindles a new Light in men. My Aim is sure. My Spirit is blithe... Take My hand, My friends, and let Me lead you over the river. Let Me guide you over the narrow bridge. Let Me show you the beauty which rests on the other side. That beauty, My friends, is your true Self. Help Me, My friends, to help you, and together let us transform this world.''

January 1986

35. The Fifth Initiation: Door to Mastership

How in the world can we hope to comprehend the meaning and significance of this great event of the fifth initiation which lies so far ahead of us? Indeed, we need to realize that full comprehension escapes us at our present level of consciousness. However, through the teachings vouchsafed to us by the Master DK, Alice Bailey and others, we can begin to glimpse at least some of what this culminating experience of the fifth initiation holds for our future — and the future of humanity.

As we continue to climb the steep path up life's mountain we must give attention to the immediate steps ahead of us, and to what is required of us at our present stage of aspiration or discipleship. But also, for our encouragement, we need to get some view, however limited, of that which awaits us at the mountain top of human experience.

Our study of this great initiation seems somewhat complicated by the fact that the Tibetan labels it 'Revelation' rather than 'Resurrection'. But He acknowledges that "this particular Initiation has been called the Resurrection by the Christian world, expressing our rising out of the ocean of matter into the clear light of day." Furthermore, Alice Bailey, in her book *From Bethlehem to Calvary*, deals with the fifth initiation as the Resurrection experience. And certainly the experiences and teachings which came through Jesus, after He rose from the tomb of death into what Christians think of as the light and joy of Easter, form the very centerpiece of the Christian message.

Today, after nearly 2,000 years, the festival of the Resurrection — Easter — is celebrated by greater multitudes of churchgoers than Pentecost, Good Friday, or even Christmas. So, though it may be incorrect from an esoteric point of view, it is small wonder that the majority of us who have been nurtured in the Christian tradition think of this as Resurrection rather than Revelation.

However, the Ageless Wisdom teaching, as I understand it, tells us that Jesus did not experience the fifth initiation when He was in Palestine, but rather that He had another incarnation shortly afterwards as Apollonius of Tyana, and achieved Mastership during that life. Furthermore, we are told that the Lord Christ, who had overshadowed Jesus during the three years of His ministry and worked through him so effectively, also assisted in the raising of Jesus' body. So highly spiritualized was that body that Jesus could suddenly appear to His disciples in the middle of a closed room — and disappear as easily, even though the transformed physical body was there in such seeming reality that He could show them the nailprints in His hands and feet and the spear-thrust in His side. Apparently the Christ considered it necessary to give His assistance in these things, so that for the 40 days after Jesus' emergence from the tomb the final teachings that were required could be given and the previously distraught disciples be assured of victory over death and darkness.

We need to recognize that the benefits of all the post-Resurrection appearances and teachings were not limited to that day and time. For, as previously touched upon, whether you call this event the Resurrection or something else, the report of all these happenings helps vast numbers of people today to realize that death is not the end; that life is not only without end but ever progresses to higher levels of consciousness, fulfillment and significance; and that we all share in the heritage of this higher life and will one great day experience those wondrous changes which will make us mature members of the Kingdom of God.

At that high point we will fully realize — what now we ponder intellectually — that we are indeed being led from darkness to light, from the unreal to the real, and from death to immortality. For when we reach Mastership all darkness, all that is unreal, and all that we call death will be left behind. We will be completely free of all the illusions of the three worlds of the lower self, hard as it may be for us to comprehend now what that victory will be like.

However, if as Masters we so decide, we will be able, like the great avatar Sai Baba, to choose to be born again as a baby and go through all stages of physical life including what is called death. But if that should be our choice it would be so because we found that path to be the best mode of service for us, and we would be doing it as a completely conscious and free being.

Another choice which will be open to us as Masters will be to serve on the inner planes without occupying a physical body but having the ability to create a temporary body, called a 'mayavirupa'. In that body we could appear physically anywhere on any mission, and cause that body to disappear when the mission is accomplished. In any case we will then, as Masters of Wisdom, be serving permanently from the buddhic or love-wisdom plane — the next plane higher than the higher mind, and the source of true intuition.

Among other realizations, as Masters we will understand: first, the significance of the three worlds — the physical-etheric, the astral or emotional, and the mental; second, the significance and synthesizing qualities of the great love-wisdom ray; third, the mystery of the human Soul.

In *From Bethlehem to Calvary*, Alice Bailey summarizes the culmination of our long and arduous preparation for Mastership in this way: "We are resurrected to life eternal and become of the company of the immortals when we have fitted ourselves to be co-workers with Christ in the kingdom. It is when we lose the consciousness of the separative individual and become aware of the whole of which we are a part that we have learnt life's final lesson and need no more return." (p. 442)

So let us take with dedication, patience and perseverance the steps just ahead of us on the path. While doing so let us not lose sight of the glory which awaits us and all our sisters and brothers when we finally reach that mountain top. In His Messages the Christ gives us glimpses of what the Masters are like and what our experience will be like at that high level. In Message No. 136 He says: "My Masters know naught but Love and Joy. Likewise, My friends, this will be your heritage. Make haste to claim your rights, and know the Love and Joy of God."

And let us heed His challenge given in Message No. 115: "Come with Me, My friends, and blaze a path of Light to the future... Take My hand, My friends, and let us walk blithely together into the radiant future." How can we resist that call? Let us give heart and mind and Soul and strength in our response to Him as He leads us toward that liberation.

March 1986

36. Music and Dancing

For the title of this article I have chosen a phrase from one of the best loved and most famous parables of Jesus: that of the prodigal son, found in Luke, chapter 15.

The older son, returning from work and approaching the father's house, 'heard music and dancing'. Being of a dour nature, he was repelled by this — to him — unwarranted and unbridled merriment. A servant kindly explained the occasion: "Your brother has come home, and your father has killed for him the fatted calf." (Modern equivalent: they are feasting on the choicest cuts from the freezer.) To the angry sibling this seemed too much. So since he would not, and indeed in his state of fury could not, enter the father's house, the father left the celebration to come out and try to explain and console him.

But the bitter son fumed: "Look, all these years I have slaved for you and never once disobeyed your orders, yet you never offered me so much as a kid for me to celebrate with my friends." (Jerusalem Bible, Luke 15:29) All the wealth of God belongs to us, does it not? So indicated the father in his words to his frustrated offspring: "My son, all that I have is yours." It is thus apparent that this son could have had his own celebration at any time of his choosing, in any way he wished. But his slave-psychology, expressed in the words 'I have slaved for you all these years', prevented any such joyous celebration.

What a contrast we see in these two sons. The older one had set out in life doggedly and resentfully to do his slaving duty. The younger brother had set out to enjoy life. After many mistakes and much suffering on a long journey home, this prodigal finds himself in the father's house, wearing the ring of sonship and the robe of glory (as it is often called) and celebrating with joyous music and dancing, while the older brother finds himself outside the father's house, in the cold of his bitter loneliness and judgmental attitude. His judgmental stance against his brother is seen in the accusation: "This son of yours (he could not bring himself to say 'my brother') has wasted your substance with harlots." Nobody had mentioned harlots before, and of course he had no way of knowing whether his brother had consorted with such persons.

What is the lesson for us here in the contrast between these two? Of course we are not to go out and waste our substance in riotous living. Like this famous prodigal, we already, in our self-indulgence, have done too much of that! But let us focus on the harmony, love and joy in store for us, symbolized by the music and dancing. Though we have not yet reached the Father's House (monadic consciousness) the Christ shows us that, if we will awaken spiritually, such love and joy can be ours right now.

This is reiterated for us over and over again in the Christ's recent Messages to us. A representative example is recorded in Message No. 129: "Many see around them a world chaotic and dangerous, and rightly so. Nevertheless, within the maelstrom of this apparent chaos is a still centre of calm, generating hope and change... Be therefore joyful and glad indeed. Spread widely the rhythm of Light and Joy and awaken in all you meet response to these glad tidings."

Again in Message No. 138: "My heart is full, as now I begin My Task, full of Love and Joy in its accomplishment. That Task is to take you with Me back to God, to the Source of your Being, and to show those who are ready His Shining Face... Take eagerly My gifts. Choose to walk with Me into the Light of the future, and know the meaning of Joy, the treasure of Love."

Perhaps all of us, in our long and wandering past, have been the wasteful prodigal. High time now to share love, to share substance, and to experience and share the joy which gives rise to the music and dancing. Even now, while on our long journey home to the Father's House, as we in real love join hands with our brothers and sisters along the way, the joy which produces the music and dancing will be the glad experience of us all. Let's do it now!

April 1986

37. Emergence from the Imprisoning Cave of Materialism

It has been repeatedly emphasized in the Bible that the Christ's coming brings great joy to the world. It has been reiterated in great Christmas carols like "Joy to the World the Lord is Come." And in His own Messages the Christ himself repeatedly returns to this element of joy. To quote just briefly: "My Message at this time of joyous celebration is this: awaken anew the Love in the hearts of your brothers and teach them to share." (Message No. 92) Again, in Message No. 100 He states: "I am with you and in you. I am the Heart of your life... I bring Joy." Best of all, many of us can gladly testify to the joy which we already find surging through our hearts and minds because of this transpiring 'event of events'.

Some esotericists, because of the rigid thought-form that the reappearance was not to take place until the 21st century, seem unable to accept that it is happening now. Jews of the orthodox persuasion seem to expect that the Messiah will come at some still future date, while many in the more liberal branches of Judaism hint or affirm that the witness of Judaism itself constitutes a group Messiah.

Adherents of the Christian churches also fall into differing categories regarding this matter. At least some fundamentalists believe strongly that the second coming of Christ must be preceded by a superhuman, satanic anti-Christ, and greater cataclysms of destruction than those that have now taken place. Is it any wonder that some of them blindly mistake him for the anti-Christ? On the other hand, many so-called liberal Christians, such as those I have encountered in churches I have worked in, believe that He already has come the second time — either at Pentecost, in biblical times, or through the development of Christ consciousness in human hearts. (This latter is, of course, one of three important aspects of His coming.) But in spite of all the skepticism and the hindering thought-forms, the great longing and massed insistence of a suffering humanity have succeeded in bringing Him forth. Remember that it had been prophesied that His coming would be 'like a thief in the night'.

Long ago Jesus described such cleavage as a situation wherein, "a man is against his father, a daughter against her mother..." Quoting from chapter 2, "The Joy of Christ's Coming" (p. 10): "There is much misunderstanding about this. What it says to me is that, if we are to be disciples, the cause of Christ must take precedence over personal loyalties and considerations. The cleavage is caused by the fact that while some are ready to do this, others are not. It worked that way before. Bitter division arose between those who followed Him and those who rejected Him. And sometimes the division was between father and son, or mother and daughter."

Unfortunately, the same situation continues today. As the Christ has pointed out in His Messages: "My coming brings peace. Likewise, My Presence brings cleavage. My Sword, that Love which I am, will separate all men, will show the true from the false, will clear the way for the new Light which I bring. May it be that you can withstand this change and accept My Light." (Message No. 74) On reflection, since the cleavage 'clears the way for the New Light', perhaps it is fortunate, rather than the opposite. So perhaps we can look beyond the misunderstandings and obstacles set up by some religionists and others, and rejoice with him even now in the coming victory of His Plan.

Time and again through His Messages He has assured us of this victory: "My hope is — nay, My brothers, My knowledge is — that mankind will respond to My Call. I know this to be so. I know that within men sits a Divine Being, Whose Plan is that Love and Justice should triumph. This being so, the end is assured." (Message No. 77) And continuing in Message No. 78: "My friends, I know beforehand your answer and choice.

Through your love — the love in your heart for your brothers — have no fear...you will choose correctly. This love will radiate throughout the world and on this you may count. My Presence guarantees that this shall be so. Already, the changes are occurring in such magnitude that victory is assured."

One of the first important changes to take place, through His leadership and our help, is a new system of international exchange and sharing. This will have priority in order to bring about an end to the rampant starvation and deprivation existing today among multiplied millions of our sisters and brothers, both in Africa and in many other parts of the world. As rapidly as possible a new and wondrously efficient system of international co-operation — based on goodwill and right human relations — will take place in political, economic, cultural and other fields of human endeavor. Also, working through men, in the process of time, He will establish colleges for teaching the Age- less Wisdom, re-establish the Ancient Mysteries, and make the first two of the major initiations available right here on the physical plane. As rapidly as we can follow He will lead us out of our religious divisiveness into one New World Religion (which is to include freedom for different approaches to divinity). A new system of education will be evolved, preparing people for all aspects of the creative life, in contrast to the narrow emphasis of today.

Through Alice Bailey, the Master DK has summarized all this as: "...the true resurrection — the emergence of mankind from the imprisoning cave of materialism." (*The Reappearance of the Christ,* p. 101) Note how the writer of the New Testament's final book, Revelation, foresaw what is beginning to happen now: "I saw a new heaven and a new earth... And I saw the holy city coming down out of heaven from God, prepared as a bride adorned for her husband... Then he showed me the river of the water of life, bright as crystal, flowing from the throne of God and of the Lamb, through the middle of the street of the city; also, on either side of the river the tree of life with its twelve kinds of fruit, yielding its fruit each month, and the leaves of the tree were for the healing of the nations.''

May 1986

38. Yoke Fellows with Christ

When Jesus wanted to give encouragement to His listeners and followers, He spoke to them, strangely enough, of burden bearing and sharing a yoke: "Come to me, all you who labour and are overburdened, and I will give you rest. Shoulder my yoke and learn from me, for I am gentle and humble in heart, and you will find rest for your souls. Yes, my yoke is easy and my burden is light." (Jerusalem Bible, Matt. 11:28-30) Let us take note that 'yoke' spells burdens, but it also spells sharing of those burdens.

In today's trying circumstances, when we are weighed down with our own problems of living in situations which often seem really frightening; when we look out on a world in crisis on almost every level; and on top of that realize that as aspirants and disciples we are called upon to assist our sisters and brothers through these crises in Soul ways of service; how in the world can we see the burden as light, or the yoke as easy?

The answer lies in the deep meaning of two words: yoke and Christ. When we really commit ourselves to His service we come into partnership with the greatest power in our world, applied to the greatest cause ever placed before us. The power is that of His light, love and wisdom, coupled with the power of divine purpose. The secret is to realize that this invincible power is being shared with us (or being put at our disposal) so long as we work under His yoke and with Him. One committed group of workers with Him have taken the appropriate name of Yoke Fellows.

The cause placed before us is nothing less than the salvaging of humanity through working out on earth the Plan of the Kingdom of God. This would of course be a most frightening challenge if we faced it alone and unaided. But when we are yoked with the Christ — whether we wear the label of Jew or Christian, Muslim or Buddhist, or only the label of 'human' — we realize that He always carries the heavy end of the load, so the promise is fulfilled. His yoke does become easy for us, and the part of the load placed on us is light. Many of us have proven this in our own experience. For when struggling alone we have floundered badly, like Peter trying to walk on water. But when we come under His yoke, and share His burden for humanity, all is changed. Whatever we are called upon to do, we discover there is made available to us both the strength and the wisdom to carry it through.

When in Palestine 2,000 years ago, in speaking these comforting words to His followers and listeners concerning the light burden and the easy yoke, He was announcing relief from the heavy burden of the Mosaic law, made many times more complicated and difficult by the hair-splitting Pharisees of His time. Jesus warned of them: "They tie up heavy burdens and lay them on men's shoulders, but will they lift a finger to move them? Not they." (Jerusalem Bible, Matt. 23:4)

Today there are numbers of people still struggling under heavy burdens of restrictions and dogma placed upon them by ecclesiastics. But many more are staggering (and too many starving) under the intolerable weight of economic and political burdens placed upon them by greedy governments and industry. Again the Christ comes, as of old, to bring liberation. And again He necessarily calls us into partnership with Him to share the burden.

For instance, in Message No. 105 He points to our sharing with Him: "Through you, My dear friends, I shall change the world. Through your willing Service, My dear ones, the New Age will be built... Help Me, My friends and brothers, to establish this Light in the world and create for all men the circumstances of Peace and Joy." And again, in Message No. 35: "My pain can be yours; My burden can be shared. I offer you both. Take My pain, My brothers, and turn it into Joy. Ease My burden, My friends, and know Bliss."

But again, He makes provision for the load to be lightened as He bids us: "Look within and find the readiness to share. Remove from your shoulders the weight of guilt and suffering. Remove forever the curse of separation, of loneliness and fear. Take heed, My friends, and do this, do this now. Know that My Love will support you. My Law will guide you." (Message No. 117) What a strong assurance. This removing from our shoulders the weight of guilt and suffering, and the curse of separation, of loneliness and fear will indeed make for us the lightness of burden and the easy yoke. Let me quote just one more of the many assurances He gives us: "Daily grow the hosts of Light, and on these, My people, I know I can rely... Walk with Me into the sunlight of the New Time. Create with Me that glorious future for all men. I shall remove from your hearts the fear of death, the fear of life itself, the fear of your brother and yourself." (Messages Nos. 122 and 123)

Indeed, for many aspirants and disciples, as they give themselves gladly and unstintingly to sharing in this task, the glorious promise of joy and light is in the process of being fulfilled right now. You and I belong in that company. What reason is there to hold back?

June 1986

39. The Life Cycle of Glamor and Illusion

The typical life cycle of glamor and illusion — resulting in bondage, leading to insight through difficulties and then to release into greater service — is told and re-told in the accounts of many biblical characters. One of the most graphic and complete of such stories is that of Joseph, favorite among the 12 sons of the patriarch Jacob. It is related in Genesis, chapters 37 through 48.

We are introduced to Joseph at age 17 as a proud young dreamer, showing his immaturity with very poor judgment. This is seen in his boastful sharing, first with his brothers and then with his father, of his haughty dreams of superiority over the rest of the family. He said to his 11 brothers: "Hear this dream which I have dreamed: behold, we were binding sheaves in the field, and lo, my sheaf arose and stood upright; and behold, your sheaves gathered round it and bowed down to my sheaf." The next dream, likewise boastfully reported, this time to his brothers and his father, showed the sun and moon (symbolizing his parents) and 11 stars bowing down to him. In addition it seems that he strutted before his brothers in his special 'long robe with sleeves' or 'coat of many colors' (King James translation), which his father had made especially for this favorite offspring, son of Rachel, his favorite wife.

Is it any wonder, then, that Joseph got into trouble with his jealous brothers, incurring such hatred that they plotted to kill him? His brother Reuben, the oldest and thus responsible for his life, saved him from that fate. But he was thrown into a deep, dry pit (how often our pride and immature actions throw us into a dry pit), and from there he was sold into slavery in Egypt. There he became a trusted slave of Potiphar, captain of the Pharaoh's guard. Then, accused (falsely, we are told) of trying to seduce Potiphar's glamorous wife, he was dismissed from his position and thrown into Pharaoh's prison. Even though incarcerated, Joseph did his level best and was soon made a 'trusty' and put in charge of other prisoners.

There he correctly interpreted the dreams of the king's baker and cup-bearer. Later the cup-bearer, after being restored to his honored service to the monarch, brought Joseph before Pharaoh to solve the puzzle of the ruler's troublesome dreams. The first dream was that of seven plump cows being devoured by seven lean and starving ones. The other dream showed seven withered ears of corn replacing seven plump ears. Joseph saw the two dreams as one, and precognitively interpreted them to show that Egypt was to have seven years of plenty, followed by seven years of famine. Joseph's wise service was rewarded by his being released from prison and given authority, next to Pharaoh, over all Egypt. His big job was to supervise the storage of surplus grain during the seven years of abundance, and distribute it during the seven famine years.

The famine became so severe in Palestine, as well as in Egypt, that it brought Joseph's brothers, and eventually his father, to be united with him. Not recognizing him in his royal robes, they bowed low before him, thus fulfilling the prophecy of his youth. But this did not happen until Joseph had been long in bondage, had learned wisdom, and given himself in unselfish service which proved to be international in scope.

Isn't this the story of our lives? Let us ask ourselves: are we still at the adolescent level, where our glamor and pride are bringing us down to Egypt, selling us into slavery to the lower self and its demands? Have our separativeness, hostilities and fears thrown us into the prison house of lower desires? In the midst of bondage are we beginning to find wisdom, relating to the Inner Ruler of our lives, and beginning to interpret that Ruler's dreams for unselfish service in the way of sharing? If this is true of us we soon will experience true release and the way of wider service. Best of all, this will bring us, like Joseph, to the place of being united with all our brothers and sisters.

Yes, and finally to being united with our Father, the Monad or divine Spirit within.

But no doubt the widest interpretation of this allegory is to be found in relation to humanity as a whole. As we witness the many budding thrusts toward sharing, joining in this as fully as we feel we can; as we marvel at the promising developments in international and intercultural exchange, and much more; can we not perceive that humanity is in the process of emerging from its long night of separativeness and greed into the new Aquarian dawn of its Soul nature of love and sharing?

Let us be grateful in this challenging hour when the Christ and many of the Masters of Wisdom are taking their places, here on the physical plane, in the key cities of our world. How great it is that They are ready to help you and me to do our part in the great task before us — helping to lift ourselves and our brothers out of darkness into light, from the unreal to the real, and from death to immortality, as together we "Let Light and Love and Power restore the Plan on Earth."

July 1986

40. In All His Glory

"When Christ comes He won't need the media, for He is coming in all His glory." This bristling statement was practically hurled at Benjamin Creme by a television interviewer in Los Angeles. Let us ponder on that phrase: "In all His glory." What a fascinating illustration that a great truth can be uttered with correct words but with complete misunderstanding. Certainly we know that the World Teacher has indeed come in all His glory. But that glory is something far different from what that dogma-bound interviewer imagines.

How ironic that 'His glory' is seen as the power of violent destruction, instead of the healing, transforming power of love. But humanity has for such long ages indulged in so much destructive violence, is it any wonder that that great power is equated with violent destruction? My fundamentalist brother (who has long since made his transition to the inner planes of life) used to say that Christ came the first time in weakness; but that He would come the next time in power. That idea was, of course, not original with my kind and deeply devotional sibling. Like so many others he merely absorbed it from the dogmatic leaders of his fundamentalist church. Yes, indeed, in the thought of millions the idea of allowing oneself to be nailed to a Roman cross is unmistakably a sign of weakness, while from that point of view the expectation that Christ is to come again "to slay the wicked with the breath of His mouth" would constitute His coming with great power. This demonstrates, does it not, how completely distorted truth can become, and in this case has become, in the minds of so many.

Not long before the crucifixion in Jerusalem, the World Teacher assured His disciples (and us): "Be of good cheer, I have overcome the world." (John 16:33) Of course He was speaking of a power far greater than the potency of any destructive thrust. He was pointing out to us a great truth, that the power which overcomes violence is that of love and wisdom. Yet in spite of His teaching and example it is evident that much of the world has yet to discover that the power to heal, to lift, to unite, to bring justice and peace is a power far greater than any destructive violence.

Perhaps one reason this is not more fully comprehended is that this constructive, healing power of redemptive love usually works quietly and progressively from within, while destruction typically comes with a sudden bang. A large and beautiful building, which may have taken many years to construct, can now be destroyed in seconds. Is it any wonder that those who look only at outer appearances equate destruction and violence with power? But let us look at the results. Violent destruction leaves devastation and ruin; the power of loving wisdom results in justice, sharing, harmony and peace.

Religion is intended to be an instrument of love and wisdom, helping to bring with it all that works toward peace and brotherhood. Hence it seems ironic that in so many of its expressions (not all, thank God, but too many) it yields to the old and outgrown thought-forms of destruction as the great power. A Washington-based newsletter calls our attention to the fact that a minister in California has asked the members of his congregation to pray for the death of one of the members of the U.S. Supreme Court. Why such a request? Because the Justice opposed something the church believes important. And a newsletter which has just arrived in my mail from a minister in the state of Arizona states: "There is an eternity, and we will spend it either with Jesus or with Satan." As a fellow Protestant minister I have the impulse to cringe at such dungeon thinking. Religion purports to save humanity. But in some of its expressions it needs to be saved from itself and its blindness.

In the June 1984 issue of *Share International* Benjamin Creme's Master says: "So mystical has been the view of the Christ presented down the centuries by the churches that many fear His judgment and omnipotent power; they await Him as God come to punish the wicked and reward the faithful. It is sadly to be regretted that such a distorted vision of the Christ should so have permeated human consciousness. No such being exists... Let us understand the nature of the task which He has set Himself. To establish in our midst the fact of God, has He come. To recreate the Divine Mysteries, is He here. To teach men how to love, and love again, is He among us. To establish man's brotherhood does He walk the earth once more. To keep faith with the Father and with man does He accept this burden. To usher in the new age has He returned. To consolidate the treasure of the past, to inspire the marvels of the future, to glorify God and man has He descended from His high mountain.'' This helps to put His nature, His power and Plan into perspective.

When this World Teacher said long ago in Palestine, "I have overcome the world,'' He was speaking of something already accomplished on the high spiritual planes within. The expression of that affirmation here in the physical world, much nearer now than ever before, awaits the great Day of Declaration, plus some subsequent years for the implementation of the Plan of justice and sharing, love and brotherhood.

Yes, the World Teacher has indeed come in all His glory. And that glory of love and brotherhood will proceed to melt away the old thought-form of destructive violence as the real power in our world. And let us not forget that we have a vital part to play in all this. For to the extent that we become His disciples we thereby become embodiments of His great power of love. What joy it brings to know this, and thus to live and work under His direction and that of the Spiritual Hierarchy.

October 1986

41. Jacob's Ladder — And Ours

"We are climbing Jacob's ladder... Soldiers of the cross." This American folk hymn was sung with gusto in the early days of my ministry by the youth of the church. Later it became so popular that it has been included in the current issue of the large Methodist Hymnal, for the use of both youth and adults.

But some of those who love its rhythm and are intrigued by its deep symbolic meaning are not aware of the biblical origin of this symbolism of Jacob's ladder. In the 28th chapter of Genesis we find the patriarch Jacob, as a young man, fleeing across the desert to escape the wrath of his angry brother Esau. This sibling anger had been provoked by Jacob's clever and deceitful behavior. On an occasion when Esau had come in from the hunt famished with hunger, Jacob had talked him into trading his birthright as the first-born for a 'mess of pottage', which was really a bowl of hot lentil soup. Esau's wild imagination conjured up the prospect of dying of hunger and induced him to make this illogical and one-sided bargain.

Later, with the connivance of his scheming mother Rebekah, Jacob had disguised himself as Esau to his poor blind old father, Isaac, and had falsely claimed to be Esau in order to receive Isaac's special blessing which had been reserved for his oldest and favorite son, Esau. The belief at that time was that such a blessing, once uttered, could not be retracted nor transferred, and that its generous promises would really be fulfilled.

As a result of all this, Esau was so angry that he planned to kill his scheming brother (illustrating all too well that family quarrels, violence, and even murder are nothing new). It was in this dangerous setting that Jacob's parents sent him off to seek a wife at his mother's distant ancestral home. When night fell Jacob lay down on the desert floor with a stone for a pillow. That night he had this classic dream: there was a ladder extending from Jacob's sleeping body up to heaven; the Lord was at the top and angels were ascending and descending the ladder. What more appropriate symbols of the many levels of our consciousness could anyone ask, with physical or material consciousness at the bottom of our ladder, God at the top, and with angels ascending and descending in two-way communication between body and Monad (God within)? No wonder that upon awakening Jacob built an altar to God on the spot, and right then and there dedicated himself to God, sealing the dedication with a promise to give a tenth of his income to God.

Small wonder that the story of this dream has endured and has inspired the hymn which shows that, "Every round goes higher, higher... Soldiers of the cross." But of course the experience of the dream, and Jacob's subsequent dedication of himself to God, important as these events were, did not lift Jacob to the top of life's ladder. Many trials and vicissitudes awaited him as he travelled on, worked for 14 years as payment for his two wives, Leah and Rachel, and as he bargained back and forth with Laban, his father-in-law and kinsman.

After many years we find him crossing back across the desert toward home with his two wives, two slave girls, 11 children, and his possessions. On the way he received an 'intelligence report' that his brother Esau was marching toward him with 400 armed Bedouins. What a prospect! That night Jacob chose a desert spot where he could be alone and 'wrestled all night' with a being variously described as a man, an angel, and a being with the face of God.

This contest lasted until the break of day, just as our battle between our lower or human nature and our higher or divine nature lasts until the great dawn breaks for us. This higher being with whom Jacob struggled finally blessed him and changed his name from Jacob to Israel the Prince. As a result of the night-long struggle Jacob emerged with a dislocated hip and a limp in his walk; he is perhaps not the only one who has been left with some physical difficulty as the result of such a struggle. But

Jacob was able to go on and meet his brother, not only with gifts but also with goodwill, with love. Violence was avoided and a real reconciliation took place.

What a lesson for us and for humanity as we are in the process of emerging from our long night's struggle between what has been called the Dweller on the Threshold and the Angel of the Presence. Let us realize that the real deliverer in our day for humanity is the Christ, as He pours out light and love on us all, and as He prepares for the day, coming soon, when He will present himself and His Plan of love and sharing for all humanity.

The climaxing stanza of the hymn asks pointedly: "If you love him, why not serve him... Soldiers of the cross?" Why not indeed? For He looks to each one of us aspirants and disciples to serve as His instruments in the healing of the deep wounds of the world, and in the uniting of all God's children on planet earth in the enduring brotherhood of sharing, justice and love.

November 1986

42. Song and Prayer from Prison, at Midnight

The biblical account from which the title of this article is drawn is found in the 16th chapter of the book of The Acts of the Apostles. It comes down to us as the report of actual events in the early missionary work of Paul and Silas. This most dramatic sequence of events may actually have happened. But, more importantly, I see in this a significant parable (perhaps allegory is the better word) for that which has for long been happening to the human race.

The story briefly is this: Paul and his partner, while setting forth this revolutionary teaching about Christ and His universal love for all, Jew and Gentile alike, were being followed by a fortune-telling girl. It is reported that she had a spirit of 'divination'. She seems to have been mocking these disciples about being "ministers of the most high God, setting forth the way of salvation." Annoyed, Paul turned on her and did a quick exorcism, in the name of Christ. The girl's owners were infuriated, because the money from her fortune-telling vanished immediately.

Like so many others, before and since, whose business practices seem threatened by the gospel of love and sharing, these owners brought totally false charges against Paul and Silas. Using anti-Semitic epithets against this Jewish team in this Gentile city, the accusers succeeded in stirring up a riot against them. The result was that the two missionaries were severely beaten and thrown into prison, with their feet in irons. But this was not the entire outcome of their act. For at midnight, Paul and Silas were praying aloud and singing praises to God. We wonder: did they get some relief from bleeding backs and aching bodies by lifting up their voices in prayer and praise — instead of voicing the curses which most would have expected? Certainly we would not envy them the opportunity of trying this kind of therapy — in prison at midnight.

At any rate, the results proved to be spectacular, to say the least. A most peculiar earthquake came, one which opened all the prison doors and removed the shackles from all the prisoners. A further result was the instant conversion of the jailor, who personally washed the bleeding backs of Paul and Silas and took them into his own home to feed them. Can we not see the allegorical meaning for humanity? For ages humankind has been bound in the dark prison of glamor and illusion — all forms of selfishness and greed — imposed upon us by the high priests of politics, banking and commerce, and even of religion. They are the ones who point the finger and cry 'communist' (or in another part of the world, 'imperialist') at those who oppose them in their nefarious tactics. But their phony fortune-telling and fortune-gaining is now in the process of being exorcised — by the Christ and those who are returning with him to lead us in the new dawn of release from our long and dark imprisonment.

The jailers are the ones who supinely do the bidding of the greedy graspers of fortunes at the expense of the needy and starving millions. But the prayers of man, arising out of our long midnight from all parts of the world, have brought forth a mighty response. Yes, the first shuddering sounds of the planetary earthquake are beginning to be heard — the social, political, economic and spiritual earthquake which comes to shatter all our fetters and set us free.

What is our part in all this? No less, it seems, than dressing the wounds of the abused, feeding the hungry, and helping with the release of all those imprisoned by unjust systems — East and West, North and South. As Maitreya has said, through Benjamin Creme: "Those among you who wish to serve the world have placed before them now the opportunity of all lives. May you seize it, use it to the full and create for yourselves and your brothers a new life.

"The world awaits the sounding of the Cosmic Dates. The nations prepare for a New Dispensation, and in trust and Brotherhood all men will share." (Messages No. 27 and 36) Let us believe it. Let us rise to the level of consciousness where we know it to be true. And let us work for this with all our God-given strength and love-wisdom.

December 1986

43. Spiritual Healing — Past, Present and Future

By all accounts spiritual healing (faith or psychic healing) has been a part of the human experience since the dawn of history. The shamans of many cultures worked in this field. In the Western Judeo-Christian tradition both the Old and New Testaments are replete with examples of such spiritual or non-medical types of healing.

In many parts of the Old Testament, for instance, God himself is said to be the healer, as in Exodus 15:26, "I am the Lord your healer," in Psalms 103:2-3, "Bless the Lord oh my soul... who forgives all your iniquity, who heals all your diseases," and in Isaiah 30:26, "The Lord binds up the hurt of his people, and heals the wounds inflicted by his blow."

The prophets often looked to God as the great healer. But on occasion they themselves, it seems, could accomplish remarkable feats of healing, as when the prophet Elisha at one time is reported to have restored a dead boy to life, and at another time healed a Syrian military commander of a serious case of leprosy (II Kings 4:32-37 and 5:1-14).

But it is in the New Testament, and especially during the ministry of Jesus (or of the Christ working through Jesus), that the greatest number and variety of healings recorded in the Bible are found. Most remarkable of all, I suppose, is that on three different occasions Jesus is credited with bringing a dead person back to life. The first of these is found in Luke 7:11-17. Jesus, on approaching the gate of the city of Nain with His followers, encountered a funeral procession where a man was being carried to the burial place. He was the only son of a widowed mother (we wonder whether the mother was dependent on this son for support). At any rate, "when the Lord saw her, he had compassion on her and said to her, 'Do not weep.' And he came and touched the bier, and the bearers stood still, and he said, 'Young man, I say to you, arise.' And the dead man sat up and began to speak. And he gave him to his mother."

The next case is that of the twelve-year-old daughter of Jairus, a ruler of a synagogue. First Jesus sent out of the room the wailing mourners and everyone except the parents of the child and His three closest disciples, Peter, James and John. Then He took the girl's hand, spoke tenderly to her and lifted her up, reminding the parents to give her something to eat. The third and best known instance of someone being raised from the dead by Jesus is found in the 11th chapter of John. It concerns a family consisting of the sisters Mary and Martha, and their brother Lazarus. In this home Jesus visited upon occasion. At a time when Jesus was absent Lazarus had died, had been swathed in grave clothes and buried. Jesus, after talking to the sisters, was taken to the place of burial. There He dramatically ordered the stone removed from the door of the burial cave. Then He gave a prayer of thanks to God, and in a loud voice cried, "Lazarus come out." When Lazarus did come out, still bound in the burial wrappings, Jesus commanded: "Unbind him and let him go." (Symbolically, is that what the Christ is calling for us to do now — to come forth from our dark caves, get unbound and go free?)

Whatever people may think about whether these three individuals were clinically dead — as some briefly are before being brought back by medical science today — or whether they are thought to have been in deep trance or whatever, these raisings are considered to be among the greatest miracles. In addition to these miracles of restoration to life, Jesus, throughout His ministry, is said to have freed many, many persons from almost all kinds of afflictions: from fever to leprosy, from paralysis to epilepsy, from blindness to hemorrhage to demon possession — and more.

Some accounts in the gospels leave the impression that Jesus healed every afflicted person He encountered. But an account in the fifth chapter of John's gospel indicates that such was not the case. Near the Sheep Gate in Jerusalem was a pool, close to which lay "a multitude of invalids, blind, lame, paralyzed. One man was there who had been ill for 38 years." Jesus is reported to have selected just this one man, out of the multitude of invalids, for healing. Today we are told that, in the healing work done by the Masters of Wisdom, this can be performed only for those whose karma permits. Was that not also the case in Jesus' time?

In the vast amount of healing work that Jesus did, He employed a wide range of methods. When He entered Peter's home and found that disciple's mother-in-law confined to bed with a high fever, He simply "touched her hand, and the fever left her, and she rose and served him." (Matt. 8:14-15) This healing touch, described today as the laying on of hands, apparently was used by Jesus in many situations. In other cases He merely "spoke the word," and the healing followed, instantly it seems. "Go in peace, your faith has made you whole," was apparently a much-used announcement.

In at least one well-known case He used absent healing. A Roman military officer (a non-Jew, be it noted) approached Jesus, saying: "Lord, my servant is lying paralyzed at home in terrible distress." When Jesus offered to come and heal him the centurion professed his unworthiness (being a Gentile) to have Jesus come under his roof, "Say the word only and my servant will be healed." Jesus remarked that this was a greater faith than He had found among His own people of the nation of Israel, so He said, "Go, be it done for you as you have believed." And the servant was healed at that very moment. (For the full account see Matthew 8:5-13.) Now while most healings done through Jesus seem to have been instantaneous, we find at least one case, reported by Mark in chapter 8, verses 22-26, where it took two treatments to complete the cure. Apparently Jesus realized that this particular blind individual needed special treatment. So He took him out of the village, used saliva on his eyes (said to have been a treatment used by physicians at the time). After laying His hands on the blind man Jesus asked him, "Do you see anything?" He looked up and said, "I see men, but they look like trees walking." Then again Jesus laid His hands on the man's eyes, and he looked intently and saw everything clearly. This is an interesting case of partial healing bringing inverted vision, which was then corrected.

Let it also be noted that Jesus' healing work was not limited to physical ailments, but sometimes included definite emotional and mental factors as well. For instance, as recorded in Matthew 9:1-7 (and parallel passages), when a paralyzed man was brought to Jesus, it was after Jesus said, "Take heart, my son, your sins are forgiven," that the man was able to rise, take up his pallet, and go home. And in all three of the Synoptic gospels, Matthew, Mark and Luke, many cases are cited of Jesus freeing people of demonic possession. People today who do not believe that possession by discarnate entities is possible, naturally consider these to be cases of some kind of mental illness — if they give them any credence at all. Nevertheless, some of us today who are called upon to act as instruments of healing are quite aware that we have encountered cases of real or partial possession (as well as instances of imagined possession).

Considering that the belief in demonic possession was so pervasive in Jesus' time, it may be that some situations have been labeled possession where the facts might have been otherwise. For example, in the 17th chapter of Matthew we find a father bringing to Jesus a boy who was definitely epileptic, as the father said. Jesus cured the lad of that affliction, but it was recorded as the casting out of a demon. A number of other cases, however, are more convincing as to possession. The evidence, however, can be weighed only by persons whose minds are not closed against the possibility that there are entities in the post-mortem state who are temporarily 'earth-bound' and clinging to some living person, attempting to get vicariously some old addictive satisfaction. In some cases these entities are not truly evil and only need information, given in love, as to their situation and the joy and light which await them when they are willing to let go.

Finally, in relation to Jesus' healing ministry, it should be noted that important as it was to Him to relieve human suffering in this way, healing was not His highest priority. What held center stage for him was His work of preaching and teaching. One morning, after an evening of healing work, His disciples indicated that there were others in the town still waiting for His healing touch. His reply was, "Let us go on to the next towns, that I may preach there also, for that is why I came out." A further indication of His down-playing the healing work is that often He would admonish a recipient of healing not to talk about it to others. He did not want to be known as just another healer.

During His ministry Jesus sent out first the 12 disciples, and later 70 followers, to preach the good news of God's love and to heal the sick and cast out demons. Their success is indicated by their returning with great rejoicing in reporting positive results beyond their expectations. Also, after Jesus' life with His disciples was over, they seem to have gone on doing much healing work. The healing power working through Peter and Paul was so great that each of them was credited with raising someone from the dead. (See Acts 9:36-41 and 20:9-12.)

Once the apostolic age was over, the work of healing through the church seems to have been on the wane. There were times, of course, when certain individuals were successful in this field of endeavor. And here in our 20th century we have seen a remarkable revival or renewal of spiritual healing in many branches of the Christian Church.

Most encouraging today is the development of what is called 'holistic' healing in many places. It is in its initial stages, it would seem, but more and more centers are forming where physicians, psychiatrists, psychologists, psychics, clairvoyants and spiritual healers are beginning to work together in an effort to meet the needs of the whole person, both in preventive and curative procedures. As we look to the immediate future we can rejoice at the prospect of multiplied thousands of individuals throughout the world being healed on the coming Day of Declaration of the Christ. Moreover we believe that many of the Masters of Wisdom, when They are openly working in our major cities, assisted by Their disciples, will lift the healing process to heights scarcely imagined before. In truth the whole world needs healing on many levels. Let us not doubt the fulfillment of this or any other part of the divine Plan.

January 1987

44. Guerilla Warfare Ended Through Goodwill

Maitreya is urging us to take our brother's need as the measure for our action and solve the problems of the world. Repeatedly, in these poignant and moving Messages through Benjamin Creme, He comes back to the urgent need to put into practice the basic principles of love, justice and sharing. He also reminds us that these principles are indeed not new. They only need to be fully accepted and acted upon. Yes, His insistence is that we bring out of the dusty closets these vital principles which have been of such importance from time immemorial.

In the New Testament we find Jesus stressing these same principles in such pronouncements as: "You give them (the hungry) something to eat"; "Love your enemies"; and "Thou shalt love thy neighbor as thyself." Also, if we go further back in Hebrew history we find in the Mosaic law this same command, "Thou shalt love thy neighbor as thyself." (Lev. 19:18)

Indeed, the great prophets of ancient Israel time and again stress these same precepts. A favorite quote of some of my instructors in a Methodist seminary, back in the 1930s, was this, "Let justice roll down like waters, and righteousness like a mighty stream." (Amos 5:24) Not so well known is the account, somewhat hidden away in the sixth chapter of II Kings, of how the wise counsel of the prophet Elisha brought to an end a series of guerilla attacks against Israel by the Syrian military.

When the king of Syria launched a series of raids against Israel, he found repeatedly that Israel's king had been warned ahead of time as to when and where the attack would come. Thus the raiders were thwarted. When the Syrian monarch began to inquire who among his men was acting as a spy, he was informed that no one was spying, but rather that "Elisha the prophet who is in Israel tells the king of Israel the words that you speak in your bed chamber." (Small wonder that some officials today are exploring such things as telepathy for possible use in military intelligence.)

The king of those raiders was determined to put a stop to such 'goings-on'. And he evidently was impressed with the idea of Elisha's power, for he sent against this lone prophet and his one servant "horses and chariots and a great army."

When Elisha's servant awoke early in the morning, he found the city surrounded by the enemy. Scared nearly to death, he asked the prophet, "What shall we do?" Now Elisha had a secret weapon — prayer! And so he implored God to open the eyes of his servant.

The Lord then opened the clairvoyant vision of the young man and "Behold, the mountain was filled with horses and chariots of fire round about Elisha." Thanks to the prophet's prayer, the enemy was struck with blindness — perhaps the emotional blindness of confusion. Then Elisha fearlessly confronted the enemy hosts. Boldly he said to them, "This is not the way, and this is not the city. Follow me and I will bring you to the man you seek. Then he led them to (the walled city of) Samaria." What a picture that must have made — a whole army being meekly led into captivity by one courageous man.

Once they were inside the walled city of Samaria, Israel's king gloated over the captives. He inquired of Elisha, "Shall I slay them, my father, shall I slay them?" Elisha had a better idea. "He answered, 'You shall not slay them... Set bread and water before them, that they may eat and drink and go to their master.' So he prepared for them a great feast; and when they had eaten and drunk, he sent them away and they went to their master. And the Syrian army came no more in raids against Israel." (II Kings 6:21-23)

In our day we prepare not only great armies and navies, but nuclear weapons beyond measure to confront the enemy. Who is the fearless one today who will propose the feast which will lead us to share in such a way as to change enemies into friends? Certainly the World Teacher is the one, ably assisted by His senior disciples. They will blaze the trail. They are already leading the way. But you and I must joyfully follow. Humanity itself, under the leadership of the Christ, must work together to bring in the new day of justice, sharing, brotherhood and peace.

March 1987

45. Commitment to Service

In His Messages the Christ leaves no doubt that He is calling us to a thorough-going commitment to Soul-level service — service to the Plan and thus to humanity. We may think of this as something new. And indeed it may be a new and much needed emphasis on something too long neglected. But this need for commitment to service is really ancient. It is clearly voiced by many of the Old Testament prophets. And none spells it out better than Isaiah. Let us look at his graphic description of the process.

"In the year that king Isaiah died I saw the Lord sitting upon a throne, high and lifted up, and his train filled the temple. Above him stood the seraphim; each had six wings; with two he covered his face, and with two he covered his feet, and with two he flew. And one called to another and said: 'Holy, holy, holy is the Lord of hosts; the whole earth is full of his glory.' And the foundations of the thresholds shook at the voice of him who called, and the house was filled with smoke. And I said: 'Woe is me for I am lost; for I am a man of unclean lips, and I dwell in the midst of a people of unclean lips; for my eyes have seen the King, the Lord of hosts.'

"Then flew one of the seraphim to me, having in his hand a burning coal which he had taken with tongs from the altar. And he touched my mouth and said: 'Behold, this has touched your lips; your guilt is taken away, and your sin forgiven.' And I heard the voice of the Lord saying: 'Whom shall I send, and who will go for us?' Then I said: 'Here am I! Send me.'"

Here we find spelled out for us the essential steps for a classical transformation of character. (In religion some would call it a conversion experience.) The initial step, in the prophet's quest for 'something more' (is this all there is?), is implied rather than being spelled out. He and his nation had reached a time of crisis: the head of the government had just died. So Isaiah's search for meaning had led him to the temple and into deep meditation or contemplation. Out of this deep probing the spiritual vision unfolded with its powerful symbolism.

Isaiah became both clairvoyant and clairaudient. After 'seeing' the Lord on a throne high and lifted up, he hears the seraph's song. As is typical in such experiences, the individual is struck with a sense of his own unworthiness. In his confession, true to his calling as a prophet, he speaks not only for himself but for his people: not only does he feel lost, because of being a man of unclean lips, but he confesses the lostness and uncleanness of his people. He feels overwhelmed, "For I have seen the King, the Lord of hosts." Similarly, when the apostle Peter came face to face with Jesus' 'miracle-working' power, he cried out, "Depart from me, for I am a sinful man, O Lord."

But the representative of God does not depart. Instead, in Isaiah's case, after his confession, he has the powerful experience of cleansing through fire from the altar. (Don't we all have to experience cleansing by fire, in one way or another?) After all this he is able to hear the comforting assurance, "Your guilt is taken away and your sin forgiven."

There is much misunderstanding among theologians about the meaning of forgiveness. Some interpret it as a means of 'getting off scot free', so to speak, by a supposed setting aside of the law of cause and effect. What a travesty. Fortunately there is no possibility of setting aside the law of cause and effect. If that were to happen we would become only pawns or puppets — if indeed it were even possible for us to live outside this law. But forgiveness is nonetheless important. As Isaiah understood, it lifts from our shoulders the heavy burden of guilt, freeing us from fear of 'the wrath of an angry God'. A realization of forgiveness thus frees us because it enables us to stand aside as the observer, viewing our life, with its ups and downs, objectively, and seeing other lives objectively also.

Note that it is only after all these steps — the search, the vision, the sense of unworthiness, the confession, and the cleansing by fire — that the prophet is able to hear the clear call of the Lord to service. Ready at last he responds, "Here I am. Send me."

When we honestly take the steps Isaiah took we too will discover what our mission is, and will have the courage to do it. Are we listening to Christ's call as He urges, "Make bright your lamp and let it shine forth and show the way. All are needed, every one... How to start? Begin by dedicating yourself and all that you are and have been to the service of the world... This, the Path of Service, is the only path for true men, for it is the path which leads them to God." (Message No. 13)

Let us joyously renew our dedication of ourselves and all that we have to the service of the world, the service of our brothers and sisters everywhere.

April 1987

46. Banishing the Fear of Sharing

"I'm really looking forward to the Day of Declaration," someone remarks, "but I'm a little afraid, too. I'm worried that this matter of sharing is going to mean a lot of hardship." Another asks, "Isn't this principle of sharing another communist idea?" Others think the idea of sharing is something entirely new, or even that it is quite foreign to our human nature.

Do these mistaken ideas arise from the heavy burden of fear itself, under which so much of humanity is now laboring? If we take an honest look at these anxiety patterns it becomes clear how groundless they really are. How, for instance, could the principle of sharing be foreign to us? The family, the basic unit of human society, involves much sharing by all its members. And in a well-ordered family we gladly provide the weak, the new and 'developing' members all that is needed for not only their survival but also their healthy growth. So it seems obvious that what is needed now is the extension of the principles and practices of the individual family unit to the entire human race. Rising to the understanding and experience of being, indeed, one planetary family is greatly needed in order to apply this basic principle of sharing to all the world.

The fear that sharing means communism was well answered by Benjamin Creme, when he replied to a questioner on this subject that sharing will be more like the way of the early Christians. Remember that in the book of The Acts of the Apostles we are told that the early Christians in Jerusalem shared to the point of having all things in common. Probably the coming system of sharing, under Maitreya's leadership, will not be a carbon copy of that experience of nearly 2,000 years ago. But certainly it will not be what is known today as communism, either. Some people seem to be so completely dominated by the fear of communism that any forward move is automatically labeled as

'Red'. Surely we can rise above this irrational thought-form or trap.

Though sharing is truly of ancient origin, we, in our greed and separativeness, have so neglected it that it strikes us as something novel. A look at a few of the many biblical references to this principle, both in the Old and New Testaments, provides us with ample evidence of the real importance of sharing in the Judeo-Christian tradition.

In the Mosaic law, for instance, there are many admonitions or commands to share with the poor and needy. "I command you shall open wide your hand to your brother, to the needy and the poor in the land." (Dt. 15:11) "If you lend money to any of my people with you who is poor...you shall not exact interest from him." (Ex. 22:25) And in the wisdom literature of the Bible: "He who despises his neighbor is a sinner, but happy is he who is kind to the poor." (Prov. 14:21) God's concern for the poor is shown in passages like Psalm 113:5-8: "Who is like the Lord our God... He raises the poor from the dust, and lifts the needy from the ash heap, to make them sit with princes, with the princes of his people." And the writer of Proverbs urges us to extend this practice of sharing even to those who are considered to be enemies: "If your enemy is hungry, give him bread to eat; and if he is thirsty, give him water to drink." (25:21)

Maitreya has given us a most reassuring answer to this question. In His Message No. 125 we find these words, "Many await My coming with trepidation, fearing the loss of all that they have loved, all that they have amassed and gained. Fear not, My friends, for the loss will be the loss of separation only, of division and fear, of envy and hate. To clear these from the world all must be remade." If the clearing away of old divisive ways proves to be rapid, it is conceivable that temporarily there may be some heavy adjustments to make, especially for those who are accustomed to living in the lap of luxury. But the gains will be so much greater than what we might lose with regard to division and separation, that it behooves us all to rejoice and welcome the Plan of brotherhood and sharing, whatever adjustments may be required.

In biblical writings too we find many similar assurances, "If you pour yourself out for the hungry, and satisfy the desire of the afflicted, then shall your light rise in the darkness, and your gloom be as the noonday. And the Lord will guide you continually, and satisfy your desire with good things, and make your bones strong; and you shall be like a watered garden, like a spring of water, whose waters fail not." (Is. 58:10-11) And let us remember Jesus' promise, given to us in Luke 6:37: "Give, and it will be given to you; good measure, pressed down, shaken together, running over, will be put into your lap. For the measure you give will be the measure you get back."

Moreover, through Alice Bailey the Master DK surprises us with this remarkable assurance: "The disciple has to take himself as he is at any given time, with any given equipment, and under any given circumstances; then he proceeds to subordinate himself, his affairs and his time to the need of the hour... When he does this within his own consciousness, and is therefore thinking along the lines of true values, he will discover that his own private affairs are taken care of, his capacities are increased, and his limitations are forgotten." (*Discipleship in the New Age*, Vol. II, p. 44)

All of these quotations, ancient and modern, provide just a brief sampling of the plethora of assurances of the great benefits which will accrue to all of us when we really embrace the principle of sharing, and practice it ---- both in personal and international relations.

The system by which blood and oxygen circulate throughout the human body is beautiful and efficient. But if, through harmful habits, wrong diet, etc., one or more important arteries be- come blocked, great harm can come to the whole body, resulting often in the death of that body. Likewise, the divine Plan for the circulation through the entire body of humanity of its needed substances is a beautiful and efficient Plan. But right now too many of humanity's arteries of distribution are blocked by selfishness and greed and lack of understanding. We have been duly warned that this blockage could lead to the death of all life forms on planet earth.

But in the nick of time the head of our Spiritual Hierarchy is not only preparing, but is in the process of presenting Himself and the divine Plan to lead us and show us the way to unblock these arteries. This will both restore a healthy condition on our planet and lead to a fulfillment greater than we have known or dreamed.

Is it not high time then for us to hear Him, to heed Him, and give ourselves fully to His leadership in the working out of this Plan of wisdom and of love? If we have any difficulty in letting go of the old ways, perhaps we can learn a lesson from the initiate Paul, who said: "Whatever gain I had I counted as loss for the sake of Christ... Forgetting what lies behind, and straining forward to what lies ahead, I press on toward the goal for the upward call of God in Christ. Let those of us who are mature be thus minded." (Phil. 3:7, 13-15)

Let us zero in on Maitreya's benediction as He says, "May the Divine Light and Love and Power of the One Most Holy God be now manifest within your hearts and minds. May this manifestation lead you to accept quickly My Teaching." (Message No. 139)

May 1987

47. The Glory of God

The 'glory of God' is a concept found in many parts of the Bible. It sounds great, but what does it mean? Bible scholars tell us this phrase 'is intended to denote the revelation of God's being, nature and presence' to humanity. This glory is often seen in the person of Jesus. But too often it is conceived as separate from all the rest of us. For instance, in John 1:14 we read: "We beheld his glory, glory as of the *only* Son of the Father."

We may ask whether those Bible times were too early in human evolution to discover God's glory in the faces of people everywhere. Perhaps so, since a study of different Bible passages seems to indicate a limited expression of that glory. In Psalm 29, verse 9, for instance, while it is inspiring to find that "in his temple all cry glory," it is evident that separation is still implied. For outside the temple too often we find hostility and vengeance, as in Psalm 140, verses 9 and 10: "Those who surround me lift up their heads, let the mischief of their lips overwhelm them. Let burning coals fall upon them. Let them be cast into pits, no more to rise."

Fortunately in the New Testament this separation (between the holy place where God's glory is sensed, and the unholy world where evil was said to reign) begins to be bridged. In his first letter to the Corinthians, Paul says, "Do you not know that your body is a temple of the Holy Spirit within you?" "...so glorify God in your body." (I Cor. 6:19-20) And in II Cor. 6:16, "For we are the temple of the living God."

Doesn't this indicate real progress — from finding the glory of God only in a man-made temple to the realization that each follower of Christ is a living temple, and we are to glorify God in our bodies? Yes, but sadly enough, this inner glory is seen by Paul as a reality only in those who are of what he calls the 'household of faith'. For he goes on to advise, "Therefore come out from them [the non-believers — HRC] and be separate from them, says the Lord, and touch nothing unclean. Then I will welcome you." (II Cor. 6:17) Indeed, separatism was considered important by some biblical writers.

But once we move to the present time, we find the World Teacher saying, "The old gives way to the new... Remove forever the curse of separation, of loneliness and fear. Take heed, My friends and do this, do this now... My Teaching will show you the future for all men, a future bathed in the Light of Living Truth." (Message No. 117) Using different approaches, He emphasizes time and again this ending of cleavage, "I come to show you, My friends, that the age of cleavage ends, the time of division is passing. From now, My friends and brothers, you will witness a leavening of the climate of the world. A sweeter atmosphere of hope will enter the affairs of men, a new call for Justice will sound forth from all quarters, and in the midst of that clamour will you find Me." (Message No. 131)

He shows us why the time of division is passing. This is happening because He is making us aware that in reality we are all divine. As He expresses it, "In all men sits this Divine Being... Take My hands, My friends, and let us walk blithely together into the radiant future." (Message No. 115) His presence assists us in thus walking together into a radiant future because He is at work, blazing the trail in "the construction of a new world in which men can live together in peace; can live free from fear of themselves or their brothers; free to create from the joy in their hearts; free to be themselves in simple honesty." (Message No. 8)

His great love and wisdom is now lifting from us the stifling blanket of fear. This will open our eyes to see the glory of God in the face of a child, and in the life of our sisters and brothers everywhere. How great it is to discover that God's temple is not just a structure erected somewhere in Jerusalem, or London, or Mecca. But indeed the whole earth is His temple. Are we able to see that we are fast approaching a time when everything in the temple of planet earth will cry, "Glory, glory to God in the highest, and on earth peace, goodwill toward men"?

June 1987

48. From Unlimited Revenge to Unconditional Love

Can you imagine a society where multiple murders, committed in return for smaller offenses, would be socially accepted? And with no indication of divine disapproval? Of course we read frequently in our newspapers about murders being committed — sometimes even for imagined offenses. But this is in violation of established law, and meets with strong disapproval by society. So, even with all of our frightening excesses of crime today, it appears that we have journeyed far from the kind of primitive society pictured in the fourth chapter of Genesis.

For there, we read how a man named Lamech (the sixth generation from Adam) is boasting to his wives, "Adah and Zillah, hear my voice; you wives of Lamech, hearken to what I say: I have slain a man for wounding me, a young man for striking me. If Cain is avenged sevenfold, truly Lamech seventy-sevenfold." (Gen. 4:23-4) There we have unlimited revenge spelled out in bold words — with no shred of evidence of any kind of disapproval, human or divine, for such brutal action.

And what of the reference to Cain being avenged sevenfold? Go back a bit further in that same chapter and we find spelled out God's decree of punishment for the murder of his brother Abel, "Now you are cursed from the ground... When you till the ground, it shall no longer yield to you its strength; you shall be a fugitive and wanderer on the earth." But Cain complains to the Lord, "My punishment is greater than I can bear... And whoever finds me will slay me." Then the Lord is pictured as saying, "Not so. If anyone slays Cain, vengeance shall be taken on him sevenfold."

So here we find Deity itself decreeing sevenfold revenge! What a picture. Of course we may choose not to take all this literally. But the point is that it paints a sharp picture of a society so wild and primitive that no restraint is placed on unlimited violence committed in revenge for other wrongs. And if there is divine disapproval, we do not find it so indicated.

These observations shed new light, do they not, on the Mosaic decree of a tooth for a tooth and an eye for an eye, "If any harm follows, then you shall give life for life, eye for eye, tooth for tooth, hand for hand, foot for foot, burn for burn, stripe for stripe." (Ex. 21:23-4) Looked at from our modern Western viewpoint, this Mosaic law may seem harsh indeed. But viewed in the light of the far less developed civilization in which it was issued, such a decree can be seen to mark a decisive step forward. A step ahead from the previous primitive standard of allowing unlimited revenge, to a then-enlightened standard of permitting no more damage in retaliation than was inflicted on the victim by his aggressor.

It might be of interest to note that this law of life for life — eye for eye, and tooth for tooth — is reiterated both in Leviticus and in Deuteronomy. And in Leviticus it is further stated that "You shall have one law for the sojourner and for the native, for I am the Lord your God." (Lev. 24:22) This safeguard, according to which foreigners are to have the same protection under the law as natives, represents a standard which some nations today have not yet achieved.

If we study later Old Testament writings we find numerous modifications of the Mosaic standard in the direction of more considerate treatment of offenders. In previous chapters I have quoted the writer of Proverbs as recommending: "If your enemy is hungry, give him bread to eat. And if he is thirsty, give him water to drink." (Prov. 25:21) It has also been noted that the prophet Elisha brought an end to guerilla warfare by inducing the king of Israel to feed a captured army and send it home unharmed. There is no doubt that sufficient research would reveal other modifications of the 'eye for eye' law in later Old Testament scriptures.

But we turn to the New Testament to find a real reversal from seeking retaliation for wrongs done, to the practice of loving one's enemies. In chapters five to seven of the gospel according to Matthew, we find that marvellous collection of Jesus' teachings on crucially important issues. Doubtless these were given on many different occasions, but for our convenience they are brought together in this condensed form as His most important teachings for disciples. We call these the Sermon on the Mount.

Many of these teachings represent a direct reversal from retaliation to love and forgiveness. The Christian Church has called this a change of dispensation — from the old dispensation of law to the new one of grace. Actually, what we find here is a radical change: from the law of revenge to the law of love and goodwill. Thus in Matthew 5:38-9 and 43-5 we find these crucial words of Jesus, "You have heard that it was said, 'an eye for an eye and a tooth for a tooth.' But I say to you, 'Do not resist one who is evil. But if anyone strikes you on the right cheek, turn to him the other also...' You have heard that it was said: 'You shall love your neighbor and hate your enemy.' But I say to you: 'Love your enemies and pray for those who persecute you.' So that you may be the sons of your Father who is in heaven; for he makes his sun rise on the evil and on the good, and sends rain on the just and on the unjust."

Thus it becomes clear that as disciples of Christ, whatever religious label we wear, we are no longer to think in terms of 'getting even' for wrongs done to us. Rather we are to make the creative response of love. (Could this be called a revolutionary form of retaliation?) This idea of returning love for hate is found in many parts of the New Testament. In his letter to the Romans, Paul suggests ways in which this can affect the erstwhile enemy: "If your enemy is hungry, feed him; if he is thirsty, give him drink; for by so doing you will heap burning coals upon his head. Do not be overcome by evil, but overcome evil with good." (Rom. 12:20-21) This symbolism of the burning coals is

Paul's way of indicating what a profound effect this kind of response may have on other persons. In any case, it will have a profound effect upon us — as we practice responding to harsh treatment in this way of creative love and forgiveness.

That our love is to be unconditional — that is, not demanding anything in return — is clearly indicated in the words of Jesus to His chosen 12 disciples just before His crucifixion: "If you keep my commandments, you will abide in my love, just as I have kept my Father's commandments and abide in his love. These things have I spoken to you, that my joy may be in you, and that your joy may be full. This is my commandment, that you love one another as I have loved you. Greater love has no man than this, that a man lay down his life for his friends." (John 15:10-13).

A corollary of unconditional love is unlimited forgiveness. This is demonstrated in Jesus' words to Peter when that disciple inquired whether he should forgive as many as seven times: "Jesus said to him, 'I do not say to you seven times but seventy times seven.'" (Matt. 18:22) Let us not miss the fine point that this is the exact reversal of Lamech's seventy times seven-fold revenge noted above. Let it also be noted that these revolutionary teachings of unconditional love and forgiveness are pronouncements given not to the general public, but to followers of Jesus, and mainly to those who had reached the level of discipleship. The rank and file of humanity was so far removed from this high level that such teachings likely would have bounced off them rather than being acted upon, or even understood. But on the encouraging side, let us realize that the number of disciples and initiates throughout the world has greatly increased during the 2,000 years since Jesus' time.

Christ's teachings on love and sharing, given recently through Benjamin Creme, clearly indicate that all of us who are on the path of discipleship (and even those who are aspirants to discipleship) are being challenged to fully embrace these high principles of unconditional love and forgiveness. By doing this we may have a profound effect on others, helping to prepare them to move in this direction. For these are the principles on which the new civilization of the Aquarian Age is to be built.

That the Christ is looking to us to serve on this high level is indicated throughout His recent Messages. Note His words in Message No. 85: "My friends, I depend on you to execute My Plan, and thus prepare the new World... Wherever I look today around the world, I see the shining points of Light of My people, those on whom I rely. These beacons of Light shall bring all men to Me, and thus the Plan will unfold. May it be that you will gather yourselves around Me in this way, that My Light may kindle your flame; and so together we can transform this world."

Look how, in Message No. 116, He calls on our assistance in creating a reservoir of love for all men: "Help Me, My friends, to create a pool of Love so deep that all men may quench their thirst." Let us exult in His promise, given in Message No. 80: "I shall take you to that Blessed Country which I call Love. I shall show you God dwelling therein, and evoke from you that Divinity... Hold fast, My friends, My brothers, to your love. Manifest that love and follow Me."

What a journey — from Lamech's practice of unrestricted revenge to the place where we, as His followers, can march under Christ's banner of Love Unlimited. Giving our best to live by this basic law, we can help others to move in this revolutionary direction. What a program! What a challenge! What an honor! Let our hearts sing and rejoice.

July 1987

49. A New Heart — A New World

The great prophets of old, in the midst of personal affliction and national calamity, were able to employ the eye of the Soul in order to foresee, both for themselves and their people, a new and better day, essentially a new order of things and a time when the people would turn to God with their whole heart, ushering in the dawn of brotherhood and goodwill.

Among those encouraging prophecies, let me quote briefly from Ezekiel and Jeremiah: "I will give them one heart, and put a new spirit within them; I will take the stony heart out of their flesh and give them a heart of flesh, that they may walk in my statutes, and keep my ordinances and obey them; and they shall be my people and I will be their God." (Ezek. 11:19-20) Next, note how Jeremiah foresees a transformation from external law to an inner law, written on the heart: "This is the covenant which I will make with the house of Israel after those days, says the Lord: I will put my law within them, and I will write it upon their hearts; and I will be their God and they shall be my people, and no longer shall each man teach his neighbor and each his brother, saying, 'Know the Lord,' for they shall all know me, from the least of them to the greatest, says the Lord; for I will forgive their iniquity, and I will remember their sin no more." (Jer. 31:33-34)

Now let us look at the oft-quoted pronouncement of Isaiah, which is repeated by other prophets: "They shall beat their swords into plowshares, and their spears into pruning hooks; nation shall not lift up sword against nation, neither shall they learn war any more." (Is. 2:4) The New Testament too is replete with assurances of a better day, a new world, a new heaven and earth. Let us take a look at a few of the inspiring words from the closing section of the closing book of the Bible: "Then I saw a new heaven and a new earth, for the first heaven and the first earth had passed away... And I saw the holy city, new Jerusalem, coming down out of heaven from God, prepared as a bride adorned for her husband; and I heard a great voice from the throne saying, 'Behold the dwelling of God is with men. He will dwell with them, and they shall be his people, and God himself will be with them; he will wipe away every tear from their eyes, and death shall be no more...for the former things have passed away.' And he who sat upon the throne said, 'Behold I make all things new.'" (Rev. 21:1-5)

Now since we have waited so many centuries for the fulfillment of these prophecies, and are still waiting, what must we conclude? That all such prophets are idle dreamers, out of touch with hard reality? Or can we see that such great insights are God's dreams, and thus will find fulfillment? How do the biblical pronouncements stack up with what the Christ has been saying to us lately?

Let us take a look at His word in Message No. 25: "Prepare men for the Day of Declaration... In focused strength We move forward into the future, into the Light of a new day. My Aim is to take you with Me into that clear Light, and to spread before your eyes the wonders of God. Take heart from these words, My friends, and follow Me. Let Me lift you upward into your true stature as Sons of God, as true men, brothers all... Take, then, My hands, My dear ones, and let Me lead."

Once again, with a message of assurance, He stresses the part we are to play: "My Task is a simple one: to show you the way. You, My friends, have the difficult task of building a new world, a new country, a new truth; but together we shall triumph... The way to God is the way of Brotherhood, of Justice and Love. There is no other way; all is contained therein. Many will find this path bitter and hard; but many more, by far, will enter this path with joy and gladness at the lightness of their burden, casting away the old, the outworn and useless, the trivia of the past; and entering into shared brotherhood and joyous communion with all that is, that vast and growing company shall inherit their Selfhood.'' (Message No. 15)

So, whether we think in terms of biblical prophecy or in terms of these recent Messages, our part in this new world should be clear. Let us at any cost be numbered among those who enter this path with joy and gladness, casting away the old, the outworn and useless, the trivia of the past. Thus will we enter, as promised, into shared brotherhood and joyous communion with all that is.

October 1987

50. What Is Fundamental?

Long ago the Hebrews (Jews) divided their Bible (from which the Christian Old Testament is derived) into three main parts: 1) the law, found in Genesis, Exodus, Leviticus, Numbers, and Deuteronomy; 2) the prophets; and 3) the writings. Of all these books, the law was considered to be the most sacred and the most binding.

So when Jesus was asked to name the most important commandment, He called up two quotations from their law, the first from Deuteronomy and the second, which was almost lost among minor regulations, from Leviticus, and replied: "You shall love the Lord your God with all your heart, and with all your soul, and with all your mind. This is the great and first commandment. And a second is like it. You shall love your neighbor as yourself." (Matt. 22:37-9)

Here He gives us that which is most basic to any religion, no matter the label. Not a set of beliefs to be parroted, but a whole-souled commitment to love of God and man, which of course is expressed in service. The fact that He considered this commitment of love to be basic or fundamental is underscored by His next statement: "On these two commandments depend all the law and the prophets." (Matt. 22:40)

This is something vital, something from within, and from the heart — in sharp contrast to the brittle set of imposed doctrines set forth by fundamentalists as the essential basis of religion. Back in the early days of this century a group who prided themselves as being the true fundamentalists came up with the following five doctrines as the basic truths which a person must accept in order to be saved from hell: the virgin birth; the physical resurrection of Christ; the infallibility of the scriptures; the substitutional atonement of Christ, paying the price for our sins; and the physical second coming of Christ. Later, leaders added other doctrines — such as the final judgment day, when the true believers are to be admitted to heaven and the rest banished to a fiery hell of everlasting torment.

Now, someone may comment that even if we agree that whole-souled love is the basic essential in religion (and life), we still have to deal with human belief systems. That is true, and the quality of beliefs we adopt will depend largely on what our life commitment is. If we are living out a life of true love and service, no one is going to convince us that God is going to consign anyone to eternal punishment in hell fire. On the other hand, if we are separative and self-centered, we might swallow some imposed dogmas without hesitation, accepting them as necessary for our individual Soul's salvation.

But having enumerated some central fundamentalist dogmas, we owe it to you to comment briefly on them, not as essentials, but as doctrines with which many have conjured. Though it may be surprising that an adherent of the Ageless Wisdom should take these doctrines at all seriously, there is, in fact, an element of truth in some of them. Take, for instance, the doctrine of the physical resurrection of Christ. Our understanding is that the Christ, who had overshadowed Jesus and had spoken through Him during His Ministry, did indeed assist him in raising up His crucified body as a genuine physical form — but with new spiritual powers. So it was, after all, a physical resurrection.

Then consider the physical second coming of Christ. While many so-called liberal ministers and others have dismissed this idea completely, the fundamentalists hold strictly to it, though they may have strange ideas about His coming to us riding on a cloud, after destructive blasts from what they call the anti-Christ. But if we follow the Messages from the Christ through Benjamin Creme (and from his Master), we learn that the Christ *has* returned: He has created an indestructible physical body, through which He now works, here, on the physical plane. So the physical resurrection has taken place, but in a far different way than the fundamentalists imagine.

Not so much can be said for their other doctrines. The doctrine of the virgin birth may have deep meaning in symbolizing the first great initiation within us, in our heart center. (See previous chapter on *Christmas of the Soul*.) The teaching about the inerrancy or infallibility of the Bible is obviously false. And it is difficult to see how anyone who thinks could believe that someone dying on a cross in our stead could wipe away all our sins and buy our ticket to heaven.

We may be able to see, however, why some biblical literalists would fall for such ideas. For they have accepted the idea that, since the fall of Adam, humanity has been so depraved and so sinful that a 'just' God would be required to send us all to hell. But God found an 'out', the logic goes, in the strategy of sending His (supposedly) only son, the only sinless one, to pay the price for us on a cross.

Nonetheless, if we are true to our calling, we love our fundamentalist brothers and sisters. And if we have some understanding of their beliefs, we may possibly be able to help some of them.

So turning again to what we find to be essential, we see that the Christ is now emphasizing the same principles He gave us through Jesus long ago: "My dear children, I would like to show you that to love God and to love man are the same; as we love our brothers so do we manifest our love of God. Theoretically you know this, but, My dear friends, the practice of Love is essential, for by Love alone will this Earth be sustained... God may be known by many names: I call him Love. I call him also Justice. Both Love and Justice are the foundation of our life." (Message No. 38)

As we read and re-read these Messages, we see how wonderfully the Christ spells out what is to be our life of service —

through love and sharing, brotherhood and justice. So let us do our best to get on with our part in the great work.

November 1987

51. Continuity of the Teaching in the Bible and In Our Day

In this chapter I will show how the continuity of the Christ's teaching has extended from His manifestation through Jesus in Palestine, right through to our present day. I have selected a number of the important themes of this teaching and provided examples of their expression from the Bible and from Maitreya's Messages.

On giving or sharing
Jesus said to His disciples:
"Freely ye have received, freely give." (Matt. 10:8 King James version)
"Give, and it will be given to you; good measure, pressed down, shaken together, running over, will be put into your lap. For the measure you give will be the measure you get back." (Luke 6:38)
"The King will say to those on his right hand, 'Come, O blessed of my Father, inherit the kingdom prepared for you from the foundation of the world; for I was hungry and you gave me food, I was thirsty and you gave me drink, I was a stranger and you welcomed me, I was naked and you clothed me, I was sick and you visited me, I was in prison and you came to me... Truly I say to you, as you did it to one of the least of these my brethren, you did it to me.'" (Matt. 25:34-36,40)

Some Messages from Maitreya on sharing:
"The central point in My Plan is to evoke in men the desire to share, for on this Principle all else rests." (No. 57)
"A condition for My coming was that men should share. This Divine Principle now engages the minds of many. Already the leaders gather and seek to implement this Principle... My

Teaching is, as ever, simple indeed. Men must share or die." (No. 135)

"Once again, I repeat: without Sharing and Justice, My brothers and sisters, man will know no peace... Take, then, the only open course and trust in Sharing to relieve the agony of the world... Know, then, the joys of Brotherhood. The Principle of Sharing will lead you thereto. Commit yourselves to this cause and know the joy of Service." (No. 133)

"When man discovers in himself the ability to share, to love, to trust, from that moment begins his ascent to God." (No. 29)

"When you see Us you will know that the New Time, the New Age, has begun, the time of Sharing and Justice, of Love and Brotherhood, the time of the Law of God." (No. 136)

On service, then and now

From the Bible:

"A dispute arose among them, which of them was to be regarded as the greatest. And he said to them, 'The kings of the Gentiles exercise lordship over them...but not so with you; rather let the greatest among you become as the youngest, and the leader as one who serves. For which is greater, one who sits at table, or one who serves? ...But I am among you as one who serves.'" (Luke 22:24-7)

"And he sat down and called the twelve, and he said to them, 'If any one would be first, he must be last of all and servant of all.'" (Mark 9:35)

Maitreya's Messages on service:

"Never in the history of this world has man stood in greater need of those who love their brothers, who love them and wish, above all, to serve them. That flame of Service and Love, believe Me, burns brightly in the hearts of many today." (No. 122)

"Make Me your own and take your brother's hand. Lead him to Me and serve the Plan. Love Me and work with Me and know the joy of Service." (No. 110)

"Much may be learned from a study of your books, but much more by far from Service to the world. Serve then, My brothers, and play your destined parts." (No. 116)

"There is no quicker way to God than through the manifestation of Love, Justice and Service. Serve and grow in Love, My friends, and realize your Godhead. Grow through Love and Service and come with Me to your Source." (No. 106)

On love

In the words of Jesus:

"And he said to him, 'You shall love the Lord your God with all your heart, and with all your soul, and with all your mind. This is the great and first commandment. And a second is like it. You shall love your neighbor as yourself. On these two commandments depend all the law and the prophets.'" (Matt. 22:37-40)

"This is my commandment, that you love one another as I have loved you. Greater love has no man that this, that he lay down his life for his friends." (John 15:12-13)

"God is love, and he who abides in love abides in God, and God abides in him." (I John 4:16)

From Maitreya's Messages:

"Take your place at My side, and work as never before. Help Me, My friends, to create a pool of Love so deep that all men may quench their thirst. My Teaching is simple: Justice and Love, Sharing and Peace will bring men to God... My Brothers and I form the Center of Love in this world." (No. 116)

"I aim to evoke from you the Love in your heart. I am the Prince of Peace... I am in your hearts as Love... By pure Love man will achieve... By My help all shall be achieved." (No. 100)

"My simple Truth, that God and Love are One, is awakening man to the promise of the future... My friends, show yourselves as men and women ready to act as heroes...filled with Joy and Love, ready for the tasks of succour and Love which will fall to you. Have no fear, My brothers, your shoulders shall be strengthened by Me." (No. 99)

The light of the world
From the Bible:
"Jesus spoke to them, saying, 'I am the light of the world; he who follows me will not walk in darkness, but will have the light of life.' " (John 8:12)

(To the disciples) "You are the light of the world. A city set on a hill cannot be hid... Let your light so shine before men, that they may see your good works and give glory to your Father who is in heaven." (Matt. 5:14,16)

"In him was life and the life was the light of men. The light shines in the darkness and the darkness has not overcome it." (John 1:4,5)

From Maitreya's Messages:
"A new Light, My Light, shines over the Earth, and in its dazzle many stand amazed... May the Divine Light and Love and Power of the One Most Holy God be now manifest in your hearts and minds." (No. 128)

"Wherever I look today around the world, I see the shining points of Light of My people, those on whom I rely. These beacons of Light shall bring all men to Me, and thus the Plan will unfold. May it be that you will gather yourselves around Me in this way, that My Light may kindle your flame; and so together we can transform this world." (No. 85)

"Be therefore joyful and glad indeed. Spread widely the rhythm and Light of Joy, and awaken in all you meet response to these glad tidings." (No. 129)

December 1987

The Great Invocation

**From the point of Light within the Mind of God
Let light stream forth into the minds of men.
Let Light descend on Earth.**

**From the point of Love within the Heart of God
Let love stream forth into the hearts of men.
May Christ return to Earth.**

**From the centre where the Will of God is known
Let purpose guide the little wills of men ----
The Purpose which the Masters know and serve.**

**From the centre which we call the race of men
Let the Plan of Love and Light work out.
And may it seal the door where evil dwells.**

**Let Light and Love and Power restore the Plan
on Earth.**

The Great Invocation, used by the Christ for the first time in June 1945, was released by him to humanity to enable man himself to invoke the energies which would change our world, and make possible the return of the Christ and Hierarchy. This is not the form of it used by the Christ. He uses an ancient formula, seven mystic phrases long, in an ancient sacerdotal tongue. It has been translated (by Hierarchy) into terms which we can use and understand, and, translated into many languages, is used today in every country in the world.

It can be made even more potent. Used in triangular formation it becomes very potent. If you wish to work this way, arrange with two friends to use the Invocation, aloud, daily. You need not be in the same town, or country, or say it at the same time of day. Simply say it when convenient for each one, and, linking-up mentally with the two other members, visualize a triangle of white light circulating above your heads and see it linked to a network of such triangles covering the world.

References Cited By The Author

Alice A. Bailey, *A Treatise on the Seven Rays:*
Vol. I *Esoteric Psychology* (London: Lucis Press, 1936)
Vol. II *Esoteric Psychology* (London: Lucis Press, 1942)
Vol. III *Esoteric Astrology* (London: Lucis Press, 1951)
Vol. IV *Esoteric Healing* (London: Lucis Press, 1953)
Vol. V *Rays and Initiations* (London: Lucis Press, 1960)
_____, *From Bethlehem to Calvary* (London: Lucis Press, 1937)
_____, *Discipleship in the New Age,* Vol. II (London: Lucis Press, 1944)
_____, *The Reappearance of the Christ* (London: Lucis Press, 1948)
_____, *A Treatise on Cosmic Fire* (London: Lucis Press, 1925)

John Gaynor Banks, *Healing Everywhere* (San Diego, CA: St. Luke's Press, 1953)

Sherwood Eddy, *You Will Survive After Death* (Evanston, IL: Clark Publishing Co., 1965)

Joseph Head and S. L. Cranston, *Reincarnation----The Phoenix Fire Mystery* (New York: Julian Press, 1977)

Geoffrey Hodson, *The Hidden Wisdom in the Holy Bible*, Vol. I (Wheaton, IL: Theosophical Publishing House, 1967)

C.W. Leadbeater, *The Masters and the Path* (Adyar, India: Theosophical Publishing House, First Ed. 1925, Reprinted 1973)

Howard Murphet, *Sai Baba Avatar* (San Diego, CA: Birth Day Publishing Co., 1977)

www.ingramcontent.com/pod-product-compliance
Lightning Source LLC
Chambersburg PA
CBHW071704090426
42738CB00009B/1654